MW01031428

Germans

IN WISCONSIN

Revised and Expanded Edition

Richard H. Zeitlin

WISCONSIN HISTORICAL SOCIETY PRESS

Published by the
Wisconsin Historical Society Press
Publishers since 1855

The Wisconsin Historical Society helps people connect to the past
by collecting, preserving, and sharing stories. Founded in 1846, the Society is
one of the nation's finest historical institutions.
Join the Wisconsin Historical Society: wisconsinhistory.org/membership

© 2000 by **the State Historical Society of Wisconsin**
Publication of this book was made possible in part by a gift from Catherine B. Cleary.

For permission to reuse material from *Germans in Wisconsin* (ISBN 978-0-87020-324-4;
e-book ISBN 978-0-87020-622-1), please access www.copyright.com or contact the
Copyright Clearance Center, Inc. (CCC), 222 Rosewood Drive, Danvers, MA 01923,
978-750-8400. CCC is a not-for-profit organization that provides licenses and registration
for a variety of users.

Photographs identified with WHi or WHS are from the Society's collections;
address requests to reproduce these photos to the Visual Materials Archivist
at the Wisconsin Historical Society, 816 State Street, Madison, WI 53706.

Printed in the United States of America
Designed by Jane Tenenbaum
Engraving on page 3 from State Board of Immigration of Wisconsin pamphlet, circa 1880

22 21 20 19   2 3 4 5

Library of Congress Cataloging-in-Publication Data
Zeitlin, Richard H.
Germans in Wisconsin / Richard H. Zeitlin.—Rev. and expanded ed.
p.   cm.
10-digit ISBN: 0-87020-324-X
13-digit ISBN: 978-0-87020-324-4
1. German Americans—Wisconsin—History. 2. Wisconsin—History.
I. State Historical Society of Wisconsin. II. Title.
F590.G3.Z44 2000
977.5'00431—dc21
00-57390
CIP

∞ The paper used in this publication meets the minimum requirements
of the American National Standard for Information Sciences—Permanence
of Paper for Printed Library Materials, ANSI Z39.48-1992.

Eines Farmers Haus und Hof in Wisconsin vor 10 Jahren.

ACKNOWLEDGMENTS

I would like to recognize a number of individuals who provided assistance for this and other projects over the years. My colleague Richard Hellinger carried out much of the research upon which *Germans in Wisconsin* is based. My family has always been a source of strength and inspiration, particularly my wife Elizabeth. The editorial staff of the State Historical Society of Wisconsin made this book better with their suggestions, advice, and good taste. Whatever errors of omission and commission remain are my own.

RICHARD H. ZEITLIN
Madison, Wisconsin
May 2000

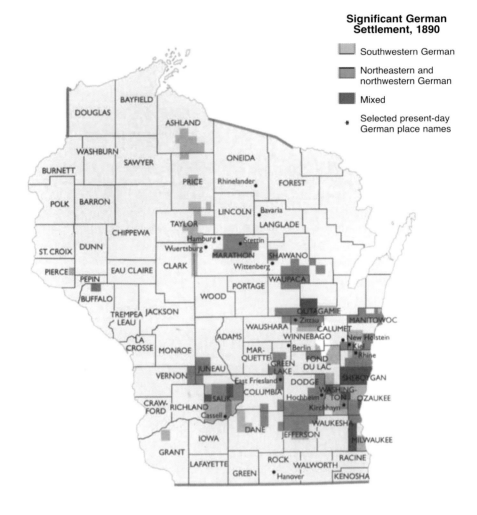

Significant German Settlement, 1890

- Southwestern German
- Northeastern and northwestern German
- Mixed
- • Selected present-day German place names

BAYFIELD

DOUGLAS

ASHLAND

WASHBURN

SAWYER

ONEIDA

BURNETT

PRICE   Rhinelander   FOREST

POLK   BARRON

LINCOLN   Bavaria

TAYLOR   LANGLADE

CHIPPEWA

Hamburg   Srettin

ST. CROIX   DUNN   Wuertsburg   MARATHON   SHAWANO

PIERCE   EAU CLAIRE   CLARK   Wittenberg   WAUPACA

PEPIN

BUFFALO   PORTAGE

TREMPEA   JACKSON   WOOD
LEAU

OUTAGAMIE   MANITOWOC
Zittsu
LA   WAUSHARA   CALUMET
CROSSE   MONROE   ADAMS   WINNEBAGO   New Holstein
MAR-   Berlin   Kiel
QUETTE   FOND   Rhine
GREEN   DU LAC
VERNON   JUNEAU   LAKE
East Friesland   DODGE   SHEBOYGAN
COLUMBIA   WASHING-
CRAW-   RICHLAND   Hochheim   TON   OZAUKEE
FORD   Cassell   Kirchhayn
SAUK   WAUKESHA
DANE   JEFFERSON   MILWAUKEE
IOWA
GRANT   RACINE
LAFAYETTE   ROCK   WALWORTH
GREEN   Hanover   KENOSHA

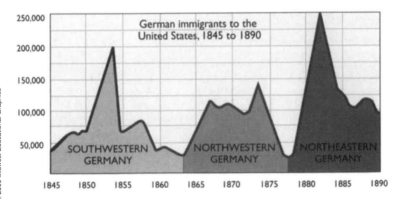

German immigrants to the United States, 1845 to 1890

250,000

200,000

150,000

100,000

50,000

SOUTHWESTERN GERMANY   NORTHWESTERN GERMANY   NORTHEASTERN GERMANY

1845   1850   1855   1860   1865   1870   1875   1880   1885   1890

© 2000 Midwest Educational Graphics

A MASS MIGRATION

Of all the nations of Western Europe, Germany played the greatest role in the peopling of the United States. Even in colonial times Germans constituted the largest non-English-speaking group of settlers. Over the years the numbers of Germans crossing the Atlantic in search of new homes, new opportunities, and new freedoms steadily increased, most dramatically in the years between 1820 and 1910, when nearly five and a half million arrived.

Most of these newcomers settled in the north-central states of Ohio, Indiana, Illinois, Michigan, Minnesota, Iowa, Missouri, Nebraska, North and South Dakota—and Wisconsin. By 1900, out of Wisconsin's total population of slightly more than two million, some 710,000 (34 percent) of its citizens were of German background, and the state's enduring Germanic heritage had been firmly established. German farmers provided a sizable and stable rural population; German Catholic and Lutheran churches became the state's most numerous; cultural societies and institutions such as the musical groups called *Liederkranz,* the athletic Turnverein, and Free Thought organizations flourished in many communities. Milwaukee, with its active literary life and a professional theater dating from 1868, was known as the "German Athens," and Germans had inserted themselves firmly into Milwaukee's (and the state's) industrial and commercial life.

Although it is popularly believed that the political upheavals of 1848 in Germany were primarily responsible for a large part of this German mass migration, the historical situation was more complex. To begin with, until the latter part of the nineteenth century there was no such country as "Germany," and few people would have thought of themselves as "Germans." Instead, hundreds of small administrative units existed in what we now call Germany. They were controlled by various hierarchies of princes, grand dukes, dukes, margraves, abbots, electors, barons, and counts. By 1815 these units had been consolidated into some thirty different states, either voluntarily or through the aggression of the more powerful states such as Prussia. But all were mere political arrangements. Religion, language (in the form of dialects), forms of government, types of agriculture, and cultural and architectural traditions differed from one region to the next, not to mention from one German-speaking country to the next. Thus, the individuals whom English-speaking American census takers sometimes lumped under the category "German" included people from Austria and Switzerland and of widely varying cultural backgrounds that included, among others, such minority groups as Alsatians, Kashubians, Poles, and Jews.

For centuries the social system of the Germanic regions remained feudalistic and unchanging. Farmers were virtually serfs of their overlords; artisans abided by the ancient regulations of medieval crafts guilds that controlled the making of almost every product. So regimented was life that each type of agricultural worker, each type of artisan from each region, province, or state could be readily distinguished by his or her distinctive dress, made of hand-loomed and hand-dyed materials. It was a world aptly described by the old saying, "Everybody in his place and a place for everybody."

The French Revolution of 1789, with its liberating ideals, abolished this rigid system in much of Europe and led to changes that set the stage for the eventual migrations. Agricultural reforms and development of better farming techniques and machinery, industrialization in city and village, the rise of capitalism, a 38-percent increase in the birth rate, a disastrous potato blight and other crop failures in the period between 1846 and 1853—all conspired to produce an army of dispossessed farmers. Artisans, displaced by factory workers and machines that now did the work of many hands, roamed the countryside in search of employment. To such people America did indeed seem the land of hope and shining promise.

German immigration to the United States in the 1800s occurred in three major waves. (See map, p. 4.) The first came mainly from southwestern Germany in the years 1845–1855 and consisted of some 939,000 men, women, and children, 97 percent of whom came from the states or areas of Nassau, Hesse, the Rhineland, Pfalz, Baden, Württemberg, and Bavaria. Small, inefficient, overpopulated, and often mortgaged farms dominated these areas. Repeated crop failures and the potato blight made calamity all but certain. In addition, a significant number of German emigrants counted themselves "freethinkers": intellectuals, radicals, religious dissidents, advocates of Free Thought, and reformers of all kinds. Though they differed in many ways, these so-called "Forty-Eighters" were, in effect, political refugees. They had seen their hopes for reform and a new democratic order in Germany dashed when the revolutions of 1848 and 1849 were suppressed throughout Europe. Many of them settled in Milwaukee, or within the city's growing orbit, and were later to play important roles in politics, government, and organized labor.

The second great wave of German immigration did not break for another decade, when 1,066,333 newcomers reached the United States in the decade between 1865 and 1875. Most of these came from northwestern Germany, specifically from the states of Schleswig-Holstein, Ostfriesland, Hanover, Oldenburg, and Westphalia. This region contained prosperous, middle-sized grain farms. In the 1850s, an influx of cheap American wheat began to depress the world market for grain and to affect German farmers' decisions. By 1865, with the American Civil War over and with the prospect of a continuing decline in grain prices internationally, many owners of Germany's moderate-sized farms feared foreclosure, so they decided to sell out while they could. Some departed for America with enough cash to begin anew. In addition, northwestern Germany's industrial centers were filled with unemployed farmers and farm workers anxious to build new lives abroad. The bulk of these emigrants came from the lower-middle economic strata; as one historian observed, they were "people who had a little and had an appetite for more."

The third and largest wave of German immigration began in 1880, coinciding with the beginning of a great influx of newcomers from southern and eastern Europe. Records show that 1,849,056 persons of Germanic extraction came to America in this migration, which lasted until 1893. (In 1890, fully 35 percent of Wisconsin's residents had been born in Germany.) The vast majority of this third wave originated from northeastern Germany, an area dominated by Prussia but including the states of Pomerania, Upper Silesia, and Mecklenburg. This was the domain of the land-owning aristocracy. The unification and industrialization of the region eliminated or consolidated thousands of peasant holdings between 1816 and 1859— thus creating a landless agricultural class whose best opportunity for improvement lay in emigration.

Fortunately for those leaving Europe in the middle of the nineteenth century, some of the vicissitudes that had plagued earlier emigrants had been eased. Steam- and sailing-ship service to major ports had been regularized, and the floods of information about America in newspapers, travel books, immigration guides, and promotional tracts had reduced terrors of confronting an unknown land. More importantly, improved postal services brought reassurance in the form of letters from friends and relatives already established in the New World.

Even so, the human costs involved in the decision to emigrate remained high, and departure scenes were usually heart-rending, as many German immigrants to Wisconsin testified. John Schuette, whose family was from Oldenburg and came to Manitowoc County in 1848, wrote: "The neighbors and friends were on hand to say a last farewell; tears flowed in profusion . . . [since] anyone leaving for America was considered as about to pass into eternity." Sometimes bitterness toward those "deserting" the homeland split families apart, and on occasion the separation proved too much for those left behind. Jacob Eifler of Sheboygan recalled that his grandfather "passed away from grief and heartache" two years after members of his family set sail for the United States.

AT LAST ON AMERICAN SOIL

For many, the passage across the Atlantic was the longest voyage of their lives. Some had never been out of their native districts or even more than five or ten miles from home. Almost always they viewed the harbor scene with wonderment and awe. John Schuette described Bremen, one of the principal ports of departure: "On arrival at this seaport we saw for the first time what we had so often longed to see, ships of all nations, in all colors, with symbolic figureheads, lofty, majestic spars—oh, how different from our inland town! . . . [W]hat a grand and enchanting picture!"

A journey by sail across the Atlantic took between four and seven weeks. Steam-powered vessels made it in half that time. It was hardly ever pleasant. Judging by their diaries, reminiscences, and letters, most emigrants seem to have had similar shipboard experiences: poor food, seasickness, crowded sleeping quarters, disease, and the joys and sorrows occasioned by births and deaths. Generally they carried foodstuffs along with their usually scanty possessions. One German traveler advised bringing zwieback, dried meat, and prunes, as well as vinegar "which will be useful aboard ship to mix with the ill smelling drinking water." Even so, shipboard meals were monotonous, badly prepared, and sometimes insufficient.

Hunger, bound up with dreams of home and kitchen, plagued most emigrants during the long passage to America.

Boredom and seasickness were the two most common complaints. Forty-four-year-old Johann Friederich Diederichs, bound on a sailing ship from Elberfeld to Milwaukee with his wife and four children in 1847, wrote in his diary: "Only a few days at sea and how bored we are with life on a ship." (For an extended excerpt from Diederichs' account of emigration and resettlement in Wisconsin, see "The Long Journey of the Diederichs Family," which begins on page 58.) Storms added an element of danger, particularly in the early days, when sailing ships prevailed. It is easy to imagine the terrifying effects of a storm at sea—not to mention the pervasive seasickness—upon peasants who had never before seen the ocean, much less traveled by ship. Of one such storm Diederichs wrote: "Doleful awakening or rather doleful waking, for there was no thought of sleep since the spirit was too agitated over shattered hopes. Stormy southwest winds have met us, the sea is running high, a sail has been torn by the force of the gale, and now we are drifting, the Lord knows how long. I am completely downcast from the long duration of the journey." (Diederichs' journey was in fact a long one, lasting from August 20 to October 13.)

But the transatlantic crossing was not all suffering and dogged endurance. Shipboard friendships blossomed, and since the majority of the passengers were young, there was much socializing on deck on warm nights and the singing of folk songs. A never-to-be-forgotten thrill was the first sight of the shores of their new home, heightened by the knowledge that the initial and most trying stage of the voyage had ended. But standing at last on American soil did not mean that the immigrants could relax or lower their guard. Commonly, arrival in New York proved a shock, for an army of con men, schemers, and outright crooks descended on the newcomers, some offering to sell them Wisconsin "farmlands" on the spot.

Of course, some of the agents who met the newly landed immigrants were in fact there to assist them. The state of Wisconsin made active efforts to attract German immigrants and assist them in their initial adjustment. In 1852 the state legislature established a Commission of Immigration and assigned a resident commissioner to New York City. The commissioner's duty was to distribute informational pamphlets extolling Wisconsin's advantages to prospective emigrants in Europe as well as to new arrivals, and to provide newcomers with full information about how to get to Milwaukee. Disbanded in 1855, the commissioner's office was reopened in 1867 at the time of the second major wave of migration from Germany. Previously, private groups and businesses made efforts to encourage immigration. Beginning in the 1840s, leaflets praising Wisconsin were widely distributed in the coastal areas of Germany. Milwaukee newspapers such as the German-language *Banner* published favorable descriptions of Wisconsin and of the warm welcome accorded immigrants. During the 1850s, citizens' groups discussed methods of advertising the state to draw Germans away from competing areas.

By far the most effective stimulus to German immigration was the unsolicited and unvarnished testimony of recently arrived settlers. Virtually all immigrants wrote back to their friends, relatives, and neighbors in the Old Country, describing their new lives in America and Wisconsin. Not all immigrants could read and write, and those who couldn't often dictated letters that others wrote for them. No matter who wrote them, these letters were pure gold to those who remained in Europe, for they contained information that could be trusted and acted upon. From his new home in Waukesha County, John Konrad Meidenbauer wrote to his sister in Germany in 1849: "You will next ask: Is it really good in America . . . ? and I can give you the answer, from my full conviction. . . . Yes, it is really good here. I would advise my sister Barbara to come over with her intended for she can do better than in Germany. There are no dues, no titles here, no taxes . . . no [mounted] police, no beggars." These so-called "America Letters" prompted hometown "clubs" in Europe to send emissaries to Wisconsin in search of land suitable for settlement. New Holstein in Calumet County was settled in this fashion when a group of Freethinkers, impressed by enthusiastic letters and newspaper reports from their United States agent, emigrated as a body.

The common route from the port of New York to Wisconsin in the 1840s and 1850s was by steamboat up the Hudson River to Albany, from there by boat on the Erie Canal or by rail to Buffalo, and finally by steam or sailboat to the port of Milwaukee. This trip required about ten days, but the duration of the journey from New York to Milwaukee was greatly reduced during the early 1850s, when rail service was extended from East Coast ports to Chicago by way of Detroit. Then in the late 1850s, rail service reached all the way across Wisconsin from Lake Michigan to the Mississippi River. Many continued to reach Wisconsin on the Great Lakes, especially if they entered the United States by way of Quebec, a common destination. By the end of the nineteenth century, railways had surpassed ships as a means of travel from all ports of entry to Wisconsin.

The welcome that Milwaukeeans gave German immigrants was often compounded of more than mere goodwill, since many brought money to invest in land, equipment, and supplies. James Smith Buck, a pioneer businessman turned historian, described the financial boost the incoming Germans gave the city: "The effect of the arrival of these hardy sons of toil, with their gold and silver wherewith to purchase homes for themselves and their children upon the country, was electric." Using their money to take advantage of minimally priced government land, and aided by speculators and land agents, Germans quickly shed the role of immigrants to become bona fide settlers, beginning the process of Americanizing.

RELIGIOUS ROOTS

Economic factors, while the most important, were not alone in attracting Germans to Wisconsin. Religious leaders and institutions also played key roles. For example, as early as the 1840s, a colony of Old Lutherans from the Oder River valley in Brandenburg and Pomerania settled as groups in Jefferson and Dodge Counties as well as at Freistadt in Ozaukee County, where, once established, they were joined by more co-religionists over the years. The Old Lutherans were a part of a body of religious nonconformists who had refused to bow to the will of the Prussian Kaiser when he united various Protestant churches under the Reformed banner. Led by several different pastors, small groups of Old Lutherans began emigrating after 1837. One group settled in Buffalo, New York, and sent back such encouraging reports that in 1839 forty families, under the leadership of Heinrich von Rohr, a former military officer, came over from Pomerania. Quarrels over matters of doctrine led von Rohr to move his followers from Buffalo to Wisconsin and eventually to establish Trinity Lutheran Church near Freistadt—the first Lutheran congregation in the state. Hundreds more churches followed, so that by the end of the nineteenth century Lutherans constituted the second-largest religious body in the state, after Catholics.

Not all Lutherans were German, of course. Scandinavians, especially Norwegians, also swelled Lutheran ranks, whose welter of synods based on ethnicity and doctrine have confused non-Lutherans throughout most of Wisconsin's history. For Wisconsin Germans, the Wisconsin Evangelical

Lutheran Synod stands out, known for its conservatism, persistence, and parochial school system, which continues to thrive. But other synods, too, represented Wisconsin Germans through the years, especially the Missouri Synod. (Most others have lost their Germanic identity through mergers.)

German Catholics were as numerous as German Lutherans, and Germans (or German speakers) dominated the Catholic hierarchy in the state from the time the Diocese of Milwaukee was created in 1843 until the present. The Reverend John Martin Henni, a German-speaking Swiss immigrant, became the first bishop in 1844, and he actively encouraged German-speaking Catholics to leave their homelands and move to Wisconsin. He also founded hundreds of parishes, promoted German newspapers and schools, and accordingly made Wisconsin's Roman Catholic community among the most Germanic of any in the United States. The church prospered so much under Henni (who died in 1881) that by 1890 Catholics constituted about half the state's church-going population, with Lutherans making up one-third of the total and non-Lutheran Protestants the rest. These non-Lutheran Protestants included a good number of Germans who practiced the Reform faith. They were particularly numerous in Sheboygan and Sauk Counties.

This religious breakdown among Catholics, Lutherans, and non-Lutheran Protestants remained constant for about a century, giving Wisconsin a nearly unique religious mix among the states. Only Minnesota and North Dakota, with a similar balance of Germanic and Scandinavian immigrants, have similar religious structures. Not all Catholics were Germanic, to be sure. Irish and Polish immigrants made up significant fractions as well, and Hispanics have increased in number significantly at the end of the twentieth century. Nevertheless, the Germanic influence on Wisconsin's Catholic population remains impressive.

A few German Catholics practiced their faith outside the mainstream as defined by Bishop Henni. At St. Nazianz, in the Town of Eaton in Manitowoc County, there arose a communal sect with strong overtones of the new Spiritualist faith that was then sweeping the United States and parts of Europe. The sect's leader was the Reverend Ambrose Oschwald, who brought 114 followers from the Baden area in 1854, complaining of "vexations under Protestant rule." They held their property in common and attempted to establish a self-sufficient economy, living a frugal and primitive life and wearing peasant dress until Oschwald's death in 1873. Then, bereft of their spiritual leader, communicants began to dispute among themselves, and eventually a court settlement divided the St. Nazianz communal property among them. Although this unique Catholic utopian experiment came to an end and the Spiritualistic aspects of the community soon disappeared, the Church of St. Gregory still remains in the community, a reminder of its founder's idealism.

FARMING AND FRONTIER LIFE

Prior to the start of the Civil War in 1861, Germans tended to locate primarily in the state's eastern and lakeshore regions, which were known for their hardwood forests. Calumet, Manitowoc, Sheboygan, Fond du Lac, Ozaukee, Washington, Dodge, Jefferson, Milwaukee, and Waukesha Counties all experienced intensive German settlement. Other German communities existed in heavily forested areas of southern Wisconsin, leading some observers to conclude that German immigrants preferred dense woodlands to prairies and other types of land. This was not generally true. Research has demonstrated that this supposed predilection for forested areas depended more upon the time Germans arrived and the availability of cheap government land not too distant from existing water and rail transportation and the city of Milwaukee. Then, too, the immigrant needed a certain amount of woodland to provide fuel and building material for houses, animal shelters, and fences. One pioneer explained succinctly why he chose a wooded area for his new home: "On the open land there are farms with 100 acres sown in wheat. . . . I do not want to buy there because I know what a scarcity of wood means, for I experienced that in Germany."

Even though many immigrant letters advised potential settlers to purchase cleared lands with existing homes, few Germans had sufficient capital to take that advice. As a result, the majority of the recent arrivals had to spend part of their first season in Wisconsin constructing a dwelling, using raw materials taken from the forest, first in the form of logs, then in the form of lumber. Usually they had help with some specialized jobs, like the preparation of logs and the framing of the roof. Journeymen builders were occasionally among the first settlers in a neighborhood. Johann Diederichs described the home he built (with help) in 1847: "Our log house is 25 feet long and 16 feet wide, and at present consists of only one room, which I shall later transform into two. . . . It is one and a half stories high. . . . We get to our bedroom on the second floor with the help of a ladder, having yet had no time to build stairs. . . ."

Obtaining shelter was of course critical for the new immigrant. Building a house took about a month, even with the assistance of neighbors and specialists. In this early stage, bartering took the place of cash. Logs were common items of trade; a hundred feet of logs might be traded for fifty feet of sawn boards. Farm produce was also a common medium of exchange.

Having secured a roof over his family's heads, the German immigrant turned his full attention to felling trees and clearing enough land for a subsistence garden and later for the larger-scale farming that would enable him to enter the cash economy as soon as possible. Most of these initial "farms" were scarcely more than large gardens. In the words of one German farmer, "The earth between the stumps is freed from roots as far as practicable, the earth tilled, and the potatoes are inserted." Johann Diederichs described the state of his farm as it was in 1849, about a year and a half after his arrival: "I now have cleared two acres, part of which I intend to use as a garden and on part of which I shall plant potatoes, corn, and beans." Clearing the land demanded backbreaking toil, and the additional effort required to remove dozens or hundreds of stubborn stumps was so daunting that many farmers of all backgrounds simply ignored them for the time being.

Livestock on this early farm operation usually consisted of a few swine and some chickens for both eggs and the pot, a pair of oxen for plowing, and perhaps a cow and a calf, obtained either through purchase or barter. On his arrival in Manitowoc County, Johann Diederichs wryly observed that his livestock consisted of "only a dog and a cat." Many Germans expressed their surprise and indignation at the American custom of allowing their stock to wander about unprotected, even during wintertime. "It is disgraceful the way they [cattle and swine] are neglected and left without protection," wrote Wilhelm Dames in the late 1840s. "Hence they lie all through the snow, frost, and rain."

Throughout the pioneer era, German women played a critical role. In addition to bearing and caring for children, women had to prepare meals without the benefit of many basic necessities. Planting and tending the kitchen garden—the major source of the family's food supply—took much of the woman's time; the chickens and the laundry chores were hers; and she was also expected to help get in the hay and work in the wheat or corn fields alongside the men, for the European practice of women working in the field was a cultural transfer from the Old Country. In fact, almost every farm task involved the labor of women, young and old, unless it was plainly beyond their strength.

Germanic pioneers adopted native American crops almost immediately. On evidence of the manuscript census records, Germans began using and planting corn soon after their arrival. They adapted equally well to the local scheme of agricultural economics and quickly entered the market mainly by raising and selling wheat. Throughout the period 1840–1860, wheat was king in Wisconsin, the primary cash crop of the frontier. Immigrant guides stressed the advisability of planting wheat. Primitive farming methods did not hinder its growth; it yielded a quick marketable return for a small capital outlay, needed no complex machinery for its cultivation, stored easily, and shipped well, particularly after railroads began in the 1850s, replacing the poor roads of the day. But though most thrifty, hard-working Germans specialized in wheat, they grew other crops as well, sold wood from their woodlots, and acquired as much livestock as they could. By contrast, many of their Yankee neighbors had settled on prairie lands that they transformed into wheat plantations. They spent large amounts of capital, going into debt to buy whatever else was needed, such as expensive horses rather than slow-moving oxen, so they could keep ahead of next year's payments on their debts. "*Wheat*," reported Philander Judson, a Kenosha County farmer, in 1851, was "the talismanic word . . . as though there were no ways to make a purchase or pay a debt without a wheat crop."

Changes, however, were soon to occur. The spreading railroad network of the 1850s had assured wheat's primacy in Wisconsin, bringing seaboard and European markets to the farmer's doorstep. But as railroads continued to expand northward and westward, new wheat-growing regions opened up, and continued high production drove prices down steadily. To keep growing wheat meant additional outlays in time, effort, and manure would be necessary. Finally there came a point when wheat was no longer profitable, and many farmers became convinced that they would do better to switch to different and more rewarding crops, especially since growing wheat had depleted the fertility of much Wisconsin farmland, and wheat-destroying insects had invaded the state. Between 1860 and 1890 there was a slow shift in agricultural production. Transitional phases in the search for a new cash crop occurred as farmers (including Germans, of course) experimented with hops, flax, sugar beets, sheep raising, tobacco, and sorghum before turning to dairying, as had the farmers of New York State some years before. Although wheat retained an important place in Wisconsin agriculture, a new age of diversified cropping had emerged.

Accustomed as they were to a diversified crop economy in the Old Country, Germans had little difficulty adjusting to the changed conditions. Like their neighbors, they tried various alternatives in search of a reliable cash crop until, in the 1880s, they achieved success as dairy farmers. Probably because of the distance to the large markets of Milwaukee and Chicago, Germans seemed to concentrate on the production of cheese rather than selling fluid milk to urbanites. Other produce was taken to market in the larger towns near the German settlements, two of the most important being Watertown and Milwaukee. Both had open-air markets similar to those in Europe. Milwaukee's *Jahrmarkt* was situated on North Market and Juneau Streets: "Operated by the farmers themselves, it was an array of stalls where every kind of local produce was sold—grains, seeds, herbs, fish, flowers, butter, and vegetables." The Watertown market *(Der Viehmarkt)* was a stock fair held on the second Tuesday of each month. Leopold Kadisch, a German immigrant, began this institution, which became a popular social event as well as a "day of sharp bargains." During the 1850s stock dealers from Milwaukee and Chicago frequently attended in search of likely animals.

POLITICS, WAR, AND "GERMANNESS"

As they slowly but steadily established themselves, Germans continued to attract more of their compatriots to Wisconsin through letters and information transmitted back to Europe. As with other ethnic groups, social "pull" became quite as important a factor as economic "push" in the immigration process, and Germans, like other nationalities, concentrated in settlements according to their home villages, provinces, and religious backgrounds. One or another of the German subgroups often dominated adjoining townships or urban neighborhoods. Thus a small settlement from Bavaria (as with the neighborhood known as Roxbury in northwestern Dane County) would exert a selective influence on other emigrating Bavarians who might hear of the community through formal or informal channels. This selective process has been termed "chain migration," whereby the bonds linking one group to another in the homeland often determined where the newcomer would settle in the New World. Although local records and existing scholarship are inadequate to document this process everywhere around the state, the documents and studies that do exist make it clear that Germans clustered together in specific Wisconsin towns (*i.e.,* "townships"), neighborhoods, cities, and villages alike, according to the German province from which they had come and also according to their own religious preferences.

The process of acculturation and assimilation is bound up with the consideration of what made Germans in Wisconsin a distinctive group or many different groups with some common characteristics. What features of their native culture survived, what did not, and how quickly did changes take place? One of the basic prerequisites to acculturation was the creation of a "German" identification. Rather than being a Bavarian, a Saxon, a Lipper, or a Prussian, some—perhaps most—Germans began to assimilate within their various religious creeds, or, depending on ethnic concentrations, in their neighborhoods. If their churches were German and their neighborhoods German (or composed of some Germanic subgroup), then assimilation was a slower process, and even a sense of "pan-Germanness" could take time to grow. In almost all cases, their awareness as "Germans" developed only after they had reached America, a phenomenon that largely held true for other immigrant groups as well.

Although at the outset their participation in Wisconsin and national politics displayed the Germans' European orientation, their involvement in the American scene eventually exercised a pervasive influence on immigrants—perhaps more so on their sons and daughters and doubtlessly on the grandchildren. Many German immigrants, especially in Milwaukee, had become politically aware during the struggle for a unified and democratized Germany during the ill-fated revolution of 1848. Some of these "Forty-Eighters" fled Germany after their movement collapsed, hoping to realize their democratic aspirations in America. A number settled in Milwaukee, where they became influential as editors of German-American newspapers, spokesmen for various German societies (both social and political), and eventually as politicians.

With the outbreak of the Civil War in 1861, German radicals, Forty-Eighters, Protestant liberals, Turners, and Freethinkers generally rallied to support Abraham Lincoln and the antislavery cause. They adopted a pro-Union, pro-Republican, and pro-Lincoln stance, largely because of their previous struggles for social reforms in Europe. Many of the volunteers in the two "all-German" regiments formed in Wisconsin, the Ninth and the Twenty-sixth Infantry, were members of the *Liederkranz* and its rival musical society, the *Liedertafel*.

Carl Schurz (1829–1906) was the most famous of the Forty-Eighters. He performed yeoman service for the Republicans during the presidential campaign in 1860 and contributed significantly to the election of Abraham Lincoln. He was rewarded with an appointment as minister to Spain. When the Civil War erupted in the spring of 1861, Schurz returned to the United States and secured a general's commission in the Union Army. Although he lacked formal military training, Schurz acquitted himself well in numerous campaigns and ranked among the best of Lincoln's "political generals."

Among the rank-and-file soldiers of the Union, German volunteers did not compile an especially brilliant record, but of Wisconsin's two "all-German" regiments, the Twenty-sixth Wisconsin Volunteer Infantry proved first-rate. The regiment distinguished itself at Chancellorsville and Gettysburg in the eastern theater and also in the western campaigns of Chattanooga, Atlanta, and Sherman's "march to the sea," suffering 249 deaths in the field, of whom 128 were killed in combat and another 56 died of wounds—part of the cost of preserving the Union. Of more than 3,500 regiments in the Union army, the Twenty-sixth Wisconsin ranked fifth in terms of overall combat losses. (Significantly, the Ninth Wisconsin, also comprising exclusively German volunteers, suffered 175 fatalities even though the regiment saw relatively little combat. Disease took a frightful toll throughout the war.)

Not all Germans, however, favored the Republican party, the abolition of slavery, or the war for the Union. Indeed, many German Catholics actively opposed these positions as well as the North's involvement in the war, seeing them as an infringement of civil liberties and a class issue. In 1862, the federal government imposed military conscription in order to fill the ranks of the Union Army. Most Wisconsin counties met their quotas without difficulty. But resistance swiftly brewed among Germanic Wisconsinites, many of whom had left Europe to escape conscription. Despite personal reservations about the aims of the war and the Lincoln administration, Bishop Henni advised young Catholics in Wisconsin to submit to the necessities of the emergency.

Not everyone heeded him. In Milwaukee, Washington, Ozaukee, Sheboygan, Brown, and Fond du Lac Counties, there were eligible draftees who feigned illness or injuries, fled to Canada or the West, or else gathered in saloons and on street corners to rant and grumble. In November a full-scale riot occurred in Port Washington, the county seat of Ozaukee County. A drunken mob of Germans and Luxembourgers wrecked the draft machinery, chased the draft commissioner through the streets, ransacked his home and the homes of several prominent Republicans, and threatened to take up arms.

Governor Edward Salomon—himself Prussian-born—was furious. He called out eight companies of infantry to suppress the mob and restore order. Throughout the war, Wisconsin met the military quotas set by the War Department in Washington, but foreign-born men, and especially the German-born, citing personal liberties, were not especially enthusiastic about serving. One reluctant soldier who called himself a "War Democrat" (meaning he supported the preservation of the Union but not the Republican administration) expressed his cynicism about President Lincoln's war aims in a letter to his wife in Wisconsin: "Dearest, take my word for it, the whole war from beginning to end is nothing but humbug and a swindle."

Ethnic institutions helped to form a communal Germanic consciousness in Wisconsin. Much of German social life revolved around their churches and internal church organizations, their numerous musical and athletic societies, freethinking organizations, horticultural societies, cultural clubs, the socialist press, and the informal institutions of the beer hall and neighborhood tavern. All helped assimilate Germans within their own communities and in making the transition from European to American society easier and more pleasant. Indeed, until 1914 and the dislocations caused by the First World War, one of the most distinctive attributes of the German-American experience was a rich and well-organized social life, often segregated internally by religious biases. Anti-Catholicism was a standard feature of Lutheran and non-Lutheran Protestant life generally; anti-Protestantism was common among Catholics of all ethnic backgrounds.

German Catholics and German Lutherans rarely found occasion to agree. When they did, they could make history, as they did in 1890. That was the year they voted as a bloc to replace Governor William Dempster Hoard, a Republican, with a Democrat in protest over the passage of the Bennett Law the previous year. That law required all elementary schools in the state—public, private, and parochial—to teach "reading, writing, arithmetic and United States history, in the English language." Because the law applied to their parochial schools, German Lutherans (many, but not all, of whom regularly voted Republican) were outraged, as were Catholics (who are generally considered to have been solidly Democratic). So German Lutherans and German Catholics joined at the polls to oust Hoard (and other Republican incumbents) in favor of George W. Peck of Milwaukee, the state's second Democratic governor since the Civil War.

Discrimination along religious lines also occurred in one of the most important and often mentioned German societies—the Turnvereins, or Turners. The name derives from the German words *turnen*, "to practice gymnastics," and *Verein*, for "club" and "union." The American Turner movement was transplanted from Germany, where Friedrich Ludwig Jahn had founded it in the early nineteenth century. (A similar movement, Sokol, existed among Czechs.) It stressed physical improvement largely through gymnastics ("healthy mind in healthy body") and social change—a feature of the movement that frequently landed Jahn in political hot water. Turners had participated in the German revolution of 1848, and many were forced to flee. In Austria, Prince Metternich suppressed the Turners because of their involvement in liberal politics after 1815. But in the German communities of America, the Turners enjoyed a revival that has lasted to the present because of the popularity of gymnastics and physical culture. Originally in the United States the group's program consisted of athletics and gymnastics, combined with discussions of current political and social theories in an atmosphere of conviviality. Throughout the 1800s and into the early 1900s the Turners were anti-Catholic, and membership was confined largely to Freethinkers and Protestants. That bias disappeared over time. Milwaukee had a particularly active Turner Society after 1850, and Turner halls were common in medium-sized and large towns all around Wisconsin. Today they are fewer in number but are prospering where they exist, often appealing to new immigrants.

Freethinking societies often existed in association with the Turners, especially in the period before 1870. Free Thought congregations, or *Freie Gemeinden*, opposed the religious creeds and authoritarianism of both Protestant and Catholic churches, upholding doctrines of rationalism, science, and humanism while contributing significantly to the growth of religious and social liberalism. Congregations of Freethinkers were widespread in the middle and late 1800s in Wisconsin. In 1852, for instance, there were thirty-one congregations, mostly in small towns near German settlements in the eastern part of the state. Other more radical or socialist German groups associated with the Freethinkers and at times participated with the Turners in community events. In 1876 the Milwaukee German Union of Radicals, for example, called upon "lovers of Free Thinking" to join them in "the name of freedom, justice, and the general welfare." On another occasion radicals joined Freethinkers and Turners in their annual celebrations of the birthday of Thomas Paine, the American radical whose pamphlet *Common Sense* had helped bring on the American Revolution. Socialist meetings often took place in Turner halls, while German workers formed reading and culture clubs "to improve their education and knowledge through . . . the exchange of opinions in the field of social reforms."

The Free Thought movement waned as the century wore on, with pockets of organizational strength in Milwaukee and Sauk City. That little Wisconsin town became one of the centers of Free Thought in the United States, largely because of Eduard Schroeter, the Sauk City congregation's "speaker," whose speeches and writings gained him a national and international reputation. The two standing Free congregation halls in the Sauk City area and the congregation in Sauk City itself are believed to be unique survivals in the United States in the late twentieth century.

Germans also associated with each other in such institutions as the Odd Fellows and the *Hain der Druiden* Lodge. A horticultural society, or *Garten-Verein*, became popular in Milwaukee early in the 1850s. In 1850 the printers and typesetters of the left-wing newspaper *Banner und Volksfreund* founded Milwaukee's legitimate theater. Musical societies were extremely popular and existed in both urban and rural German communities; singing groups like the *Liederkranz* brought German communities a degree of culture generally not found elsewhere. So popular and influential were these *Musik-Vereine* in Milwaukee that the city became renowned for a time as the center of the fine arts in the Middle West, before it was superseded by Chicago. These various groups not only provided outlets for social mingling, but also served as vehicles for keeping the German language actively in use among the children and grandchildren of immigrants.

Ubiquitous taverns and beer gardens likewise played a conspicuous part in the social life of Wisconsin Germans. While beer halls were not uniquely German, the way Germans used them made this informal institution function as an integral part of community affairs. In German settlements and urban neighborhoods the beer hall served as a meeting place or ballroom, a "convivial atmosphere for turning strangers into friends." Entire families visited German taverns, especially on Sundays (the so-called "Continental Sunday"). There they had a meal, played cards, and sometimes engaged in organized sports. On the other hand, Yankee taverns, according to contemporary accounts, offered scenes of "ready drunkenness" and were places where people (mostly men) bought "rounds" for their friends, drank their liquor standing up, and quickly went about their business. Drunkenness was a fixture of German taverns as well, and alcoholism was a common destructive force in Germanic communities. Wisconsin's so-called "tavern culture," in which the tavern became a meeting place and social center for a neighborhood, evolved out of this composite and eventually pervaded most of the state. It survived Prohibition (1919–1933) and to this day continues in cities and hamlets throughout the state, although the tradition diminished in the late twentieth century largely because of reduced sales of alcoholic beverages and increased cultural homogeneity.

One byproduct of this vibrant and extensive Germanic network was the introduction of such European-born doctrines as Marxism, the class struggle, workers' right to organize, and a widespread acceptance of the tenets of socialism. By the 1860s, German-born workers constituted almost half of Milwaukee's wage earners. They predominated in the brewing, carpentry, cigarmaking, and tailoring industries and were distributed more or less evenly throughout the rest of the industrial work force.

German-born organizers were in the vanguard of the long struggle for workers' right to organize in Wisconsin's shops and factories, and their influence extended well into the twentieth century. Prominent among German activists was Robert Schilling (1843–1922), born in Saxony, who came to Wisconsin in 1880, initially to edit a German-language paper but before long to organize Milwaukee's industrial workers for the Knights of Labor. In 1886 he led the Knights to the zenith of their success in Wisconsin, when labor candidates swept all political offices in Milwaukee County. One of Schilling's rivals on the left was Paul Grottkau (1846–1898), Berlin-born, a fiery orator and lifelong Socialist who arrived in Milwaukee in 1883, where for eight years he edited the *Arbeiter Zeitung* ("Workers Newspaper"), agitated for workers' right to organize, and was widely reviled by corporate management as an "anarchist." Both Grottkau and Schilling helped to organize a massive strike for an eight-hour workday, culminating in the so-called "Bay View Massacre" of May 5, 1886, in which a Wisconsin militia unit, summoned by the governor to maintain order, killed seven people, including five striking workers. Most of these strikers were Polish. (Grottkau was arrested and received a year in jail for his role in the affair.) A similar tragedy was averted at a gathering of German workers at a west side beer garden on the same day.

The careers of Schilling, Grottkau, and other German editors, organizers, and reformers left an indelible stamp on the labor movement in Wisconsin. Among their successors on the left were Frank J. Weber (1849–1943), the driving force behind the founding of the Wisconsin State Federation of Labor in 1893 and a Socialist member of the Wisconsin legislature, 1907–1912 and 1923–1926; and Victor L. Berger (1860–1929), the Socialist editor of Milwaukee's German-language *Vorwaerts* ("Forward"), who in 1918 was elected to Congress. (He had already served a term from 1910 to 1912 and was the first Socialist to sit in the House of Representatives.) Because his English-language paper, the Milwaukee *Leader,* opposed American participation in the Great War, Berger had been indicted for conspiring to violate the federal Espionage Act even before he was elected in 1918. The House denied him his seat, and in 1919 Berger was sentenced to twenty years in prison. Then in 1921 the U.S. Supreme Court overturned his conviction, enabling Berger to stand for reelection. Ultimately he served in the House from 1923 to 1929, where he articulated a liberal-socialist agenda and earned the respect of his peers.

Berger's first election to Congress in 1910 coincided with a virtual Socialist takeover of Milwaukee city and county government that year. In response to corruption scandals in government, voters installed Socialists in the mayor's office and the other city offices and on the city council and the county board. Germans, of course, were most responsible for the success; but progressive- and socialist-minded Poles and others cast their ballots for reform as well. (Corruption of the sort suffered in Milwaukee in 1910 was common in America's largest cities.) The kinds of changes promised by the German-inspired Socialists had a broad appeal.

The principal figure in Milwaukee from 1910 to 1912 was the mayor, Emil Seidel (1864–1947), whose parents were German immigrants but who himself had been born in Pennsylvania and brought to Milwaukee as an infant. As promised in his campaign, he created a bureau of "economy and efficiency" to clean up government. It brought about improved sanitary facilities, factory inspection, health measures of all sorts, reduction in the costs of paving streets with asphalt (replacing dirt and cinders), better schools, and more publicly supported entertainment and recreation. The improvements in sanitary conditions led to popular use of the phrase "sewer socialism" to describe what was going on in Milwaukee—achievements widely associated with the city's Germanic majority. This brand of socialism drew favorable comment from around the country and the world.

The Socialists lost in 1912, then regained Milwaukee's executive branch in 1916 and held on to it with only an eight-year break until 1960—a unique chapter in the governance of a major American city. From 1916 until 1940, Daniel Hoan (1881–1961), of Irish, German, and English background, presided as mayor, supported by the city's immense Germanic and Polish working class. The Catholic hierarchy at first warned against the Socialist party, then accommodated itself as time went on. From 1948 until 1960, Frank P. Zeidler (born in 1912), a German American, lifelong student of government, and traditional German Lutheran, held the helm as the nation's last major Socialist officeholder. Zeidler's interest in history and Germanism (he was fairly fluent in the language) has continued to the present and has helped spark the modern revival of popular interest in Wisconsin and Milwaukee's Germanic past.

INDUSTRY, EDUCATION, AND PROPRIETORSHIP OF THE LAND

The Milwaukee industries and businesses that the German-inspired labor movement challenged were themselves heavily Germanic. By the end of the nineteenth century, German owners and operators dominated Milwaukee's flour mills, breweries, tanneries, printing and engraving shops, and machine shops. Yankees, who got Wisconsin going, retained their sway over the financial and commercial aspects of Milwaukee (and Wisconsin) business life, but as Germans succeeded in their endeavors, these Yankee elements took them on as partners and appointed them as officers and board members in banks and businesses.

Grain was big business in Milwaukee because of its excellent rail and water transportation connections. By 1892, Germans controlled most of the milling in the city. John B. A. Kern, a Bavarian who came to Milwaukee in 1859 from Philadelphia, owned the largest mill, which produced flour under the name of Eagle. Other mills were those of C. Manegold and Son; Faist, Kraus and Company; F. H. Magdeburg and Company; and B. Stern and Son. Germans also controlled leather tanning, another big business in a city where meatpacking produced hides. The state's lumber industry in turn produced the bark necessary for tanning (chemical replacements for bark were developed around the turn of the century). Guido Pfister and Fred

Vogel, both Germans, led in tanning, and Pfister's name lives on in the Milwaukee hotel.

Brewing and German brewers put Milwaukee on the ethnic map around the country. But it was not only their beer that did it; it was also their advertising. Milwaukee breweries—Pabst, Schlitz, Miller, and Best were the Germanic names everyone recognized—could produce far more beer than Milwaukeeans could consume. After the famed Chicago Fire in October 1871, Chicago's breweries mostly lay in ruins. So Milwaukee's breweries stepped in and learned how to market their product outside their own area. They—especially Pabst—refined advertising and promotion techniques and developed containers in which beer could be shipped safely, thus taking the lead in national distribution of a product that previously had been known only regionally. A century later, the tables turned again, and regional and local beers began to regain the market, spelling an end to the Schlitz and Pabst brands.

What happened in Milwaukee's industries and businesses with respect to Germans happened elsewhere in Wisconsin where Germanic immigrants settled in significant numbers. In all parts of the state, in middle-sized and small cities like Sheboygan, Manitowoc, Port Washington, West Bend, Watertown, La Crosse, Wausau, and in villages and hamlets where Germans predominated, manufacturing and commercial institutions took on an ethnic cast.

Similarly, Germanic influences were felt in schooling, especially concerning instruction in the mother tongue. Germans contributed funds to establish and maintain private German-language schools. (The German-English Academy in Milwaukee was especially well known, as was the school run by Mathilde Anneke, a Forty-Eighter.) And both German Catholics and German Lutherans established parochial schools whose principal language was often German. The students learned some English in the classroom, but they heard and spoke German at home, on the playground, in church, and in many of the businesses they patronized. (Relatively fewer Norwegian and Polish churches also had parochial schools in which their native tongues were spoken.) German speakers' loyalty to their native tongue was almost universal at first but changed dramatically in the twentieth century as a result of the unpopularity of all things Germanic in the wake of World War I. In the words of one nineteenth-century immigrant, "All would like to have their children read and write in German, and to receive religious instruction in that language." Germans brought with them a distinct regard for learning, and many immigrants had attained relatively high levels of education in their homeland. Even in remote rural areas, a surprisingly large number of *lateinische Bauern,* or well-educated "Latin farmers," could be found in the middle and late 1800s.

These well-educated Wisconsin Germans quickly earned the respect of the intellectual and political elite in the United States, since Germany led the world in developing institutions of higher education in the nineteenth century, and it was a badge of distinction for an American scholar to have studied at a German university. Leading American institutions such as Harvard and Johns Hopkins began patterning their courses of study after German models and introduced postgraduate schools along German lines. The young University of Wisconsin in Madison (founded in 1849) followed suit in the late 1800s. By the time of the Civil War, it had introduced German-language studies into the curriculum as an alternative to the classic Greek and Latin requirements.

German ideas about education also helped shape Wisconsin's school systems. The United States' first kindergarten—an obvious German import—began as a short-lived, private undertaking in Watertown in 1856 by Margarethe Meyer Schurz (wife of Carl Schurz), for the benefit of her daughter, Agatha. Heavily German Manitowoc was the first community to support a kindergarten publicly, in 1873. German prototypes extended beyond classes for young children. Ideas employed in Germany about vocational education coupled with the educational reforms suggested by John Dewey ("learn by doing") led to the establishment of county-level high schools for rural boys and girls in 1901–1902 and to the formation of the nation's first statewide adult and vocational school system in 1911.

German ideas also heavily influenced Wisconsin government around 1900, when the Progressive Era took hold. The famed "Wisconsin Idea" was traced in part by its de-facto founder, Charles McCarthy, to examples he found in Germany in the early 1900s, and he credited Wisconsin's receptiveness for these reform ideas to its being "fundamentally a German state." It would be wrong to assert that the Wisconsin Idea is a German idea, but it embodied some German concepts. Scholars agree that it involved a "scientific" laboratory for drafting legislation and gathering ideas—the Legislative Reference Library. It also involved heavy cooperation in this process with the University of Wisconsin and its faculty, who advised about legislation and sat on commissions. And it involved independent, nonpartisan government commissions that oversaw such entities as railroads, utilities, and conservation.

One important attitude that German settlers displayed in Wisconsin was a feeling of proprietorship toward their new land. Conditioned by European memories, they looked on the land as the foundation, the basis for an estate that could be passed on to succeeding generations, a viewpoint that assured stability of residence in specific localities. Germans were literally unwilling to sell their farms and move on, as did so many other Americans. As one historian observes, "Once in possession of a tract of land, the German tended to hold on, through good years and bad years, as if his farm were the one piece of land in the world for him and his." Yankees, on the other hand, tended to think of their land as a resource to be exploited, to be used for speculation, perhaps to be sold. "They did not give back to the soil those elements necessary to maintain its fertility," observed a Washington County historian in comparing Yankee and German farmers. "For this reason Wisconsin was fortunate to be favored so much by the German immigrant farmer who came here to stay. . . ." According to A. F. Evast, writing in 1889, German farmers taught their American cousins the methods of "rational farming," by learning about the peculiarities of the farm and livestock, by rotating crops, by weeding, trimming, pruning, and conserving the soil and all that grew upon it. German farmers were famous for saving the droppings of their livestock and applying it liberally to their fields—a practice summarized in several old German folk sayings. ("The manure pit is the farmer's gold pit," and "Where there is manure there is Christ.") Above all, German farmers eschewed speculation, preferring to invest their savings in neighboring fields with which they were intimately familiar. Avoiding risks and adventurous experiments necessitating loans, Germans were content to cultivate their small plots intensively and to progress slowly but steadily toward stability and success, all the while incorporating American advances in machinery and farming technology.

Caring for livestock seems to have been related to German attitudes toward sound farming practices. Settlers who arrived with enough capital soon constructed barns to house their livestock. Johann Kerler expressed the general feeling when he wrote in 1849: "I could not bring myself to leave cattle out in the open during the cold months as the milk would freeze in the cow's udder."

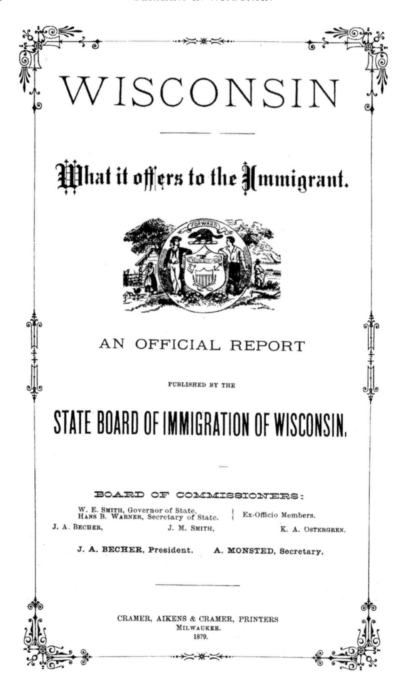

WISCONSIN

𝕸𝖍𝖆𝖙 𝖎𝖙 𝖔𝖋𝖋𝖊𝖗𝖘 𝖙𝖔 𝖙𝖍𝖊 𝕴𝖒𝖒𝖎𝖌𝖗𝖆𝖓𝖙.

AN OFFICIAL REPORT

PUBLISHED BY THE

STATE BOARD OF IMMIGRATION OF WISCONSIN,

BOARD OF COMMISSIONERS:

W. E. SMITH, Governor of State.   } Ex-Officio Members.
HANS B. WARNER, Secretary of State.   }

J. A. BECHER,   J. M. SMITH,   K. A. OSTERGREN.

J. A. BECHER, President.   A. MONSTED, Secretary.

CRAMER, AIKENS & CRAMER, PRINTERS
MILWAUKEE.
1879.

Title pages, in English and German, of pamphlets advertising opportunities for immigrants in Wisconsin. The pamphlets are among the rare books in the collections of the State Historical Society of Wisconsin.

Wisconsin.

Ein Bericht über

Bevölkerung, Boden, Klima, Handel

—und die—

industriellen Verhältnisse

dieses Staates im Nordwesten der nordamericanischen Union.

Veröffentlicht von der

Staats-Einwanderungs-Behörde.

(Siebente Auflage.)

Mitglieder der Behörde.

W. E. Smith, Staats-Gouverneur. }
Hans B. Warner, Staats-Secretär. } Ex-Officio.
J. A Becher, J. M. Smith, K. A. Ostergren.

J. A. Becher, Präsident.   **Henry Baetz,** Secretär.

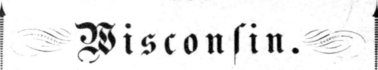

Exemplare dieser Broschüre sind kosten- und portofrei zu beziehen durch den Secretär
Henry Baetz,
144 Clinton-Straße, Milwaukee, Wis.

1881.

Schnellpressendruck des „Herold", Milwaukee, Wis.

WHi(X3)25839

Log home built by Christian Turck of Germantown, Washington County. Turck had immigrated from the German state of Nassau in 1846. The structure is preserved as part of the German complex at Old World Wisconsin near Eagle in Waukesha County.

WHi(K91)202

Members of the Krueger family harvesting sorghum on their Dodge County farm, 1901.

WHi(K91)400

Jennie Krueger of rural Watertown, Dodge County, pictured c. 1910 in her grand-mother's "immigrant dress" and wooden slippers. To her right are an old spinning wheel, a yarn holder, and a basket of raw wool.

WHi(K91)410

Jennie's grandparents, Mary (Goetsch) and August Krueger, harvesting grain on their Dodge County farm around 1900.

WHi(X3)32529

Open-air "pig fair" in the heavily German city of Watertown in northern Dodge County, 1923.

WHi(T355)62

Horse-drawn produce at a Milwaukee loading dock, c. 1910.

WHi(X3)32467

The Sauk City Dramatic Company—Germans all—in costume for their performance of *Der Wirwass* (Chaos) in 1904.

Whi(X3)28766

German businessmen at their annual fishing and beer picnic on the Lake Michigan shore near Sheboygan Falls, c. 1900.

VMA/329152

Anna Sauthoff of Madison, photographed about 1875 in her Turnverein outfit.

Lang's illustrated handbook of Turnverein exercises, published in Chicago in 1876 and widely employed throughout Wisconsin. The original is in the Visual Materials Archive of the State Historical Society of Wisconsin.

Whi(X3)23316

This Milwaukee Turnverein group won five prizes at the 1880 international Turner competition in Germany.

WHi(X3)17708

Classic photo of a German men's singing society in Wausau, Marathon County, just prior to World War I.

VMA/Harry Keith collection

Schlitz Brewing Co. workers enjoying a holiday weekend at an unnamed Wisconsin resort, c. 1910.

ADAPTATION AND CHANGE

It is small wonder that the results of German frugality, careful husbandry, a willingness to adopt new equipment and practices, and plain hard work were evident by the time of the state census of 1905. By then, farms in the towns of Herman and Theresa in Dodge County—an area that had been extremely poor and heavily German in the pioneer era—were discovered to have achieved the highest per-unit evaluation in the state. By contrast, Yankee townships in the same county, which had led in individual farm valuation for nearly half a century, had declined in value. In Dodge County, as elsewhere, the industry, intelligence, and methodical progress of German farmers were manifested in the census and other public records.

Other evidences of Germanic material culture brought to Wisconsin are difficult to come by. After all, immigrants traveled light. Bedding, a change of clothing, some tools, wooden shoes, wooden slippers called *pantoffel,* and high hopes were about all that could be carried. It was probably just as well that the immigrant did not bring an extensive wardrobe, for undoubtedly there was nativist pressure on them to conform to American dress—felt especially by the younger generation anxious to become Americanized. Writing to his mother in Germany in 1852, one young man said, "Dear mother, you ought to see me now with my new clothes, long black coat, black vest and trousers, choker, black silk hat, and my hair parted not only on the top but also on the back of the head! I suppose it looks funny, but then you must do as the Romans, or they will point at you: 'Look there, that Dutchman.'"

As with other immigrant groups, the Americanization of second-generation Germans progressed rapidly because younger settlers, especially, yearned to adopt and conform to American customs. Likewise, the designs of buildings and interior home furnishings gradually came under the influence of American styles, growing stronger with each decade as low-priced, mass-produced goods became more readily available. As early as 1850, Ernst Frank wrote, "The furnishing of homes in America is the same everywhere." But Frank was writing about urban areas. Mass-produced goods and American tastes were slower to arrive in isolated areas.

Material evidences of German culture hardly disappeared immediately upon the immigrant's arrival, but the processes of adaptation and change did begin swiftly. During the initial pioneer stage the immigrant had little time to express true Germanness, since basic physical survival was the paramount concern. Germans often followed the advice of guidebooks, copied their earlier neighbors' log cabins, and planted locally tested crops such as corn. Not until they had reached a level of physical and economic security were some Germans able to exercise their ethnic preferences in housing and farm buildings. And some of these immigrants then displayed certain preferences for a return to older, long-established folkways—what has been termed "cultural rebound."

The ability to achieve that goal often depended on the presence of skilled, mature craftsmen—men and women alike—who had learned techniques and designs in the Old Country. Many immigrant clusters included such experts who made all manner of practical and decorative objects (furniture, textiles, utensils, tools) as well as buildings. Isolation frequently demanded that they create something almost immediately after they had arrived, and they put their skills to use on behalf of their entire communities, not just for their own families. In these cases, "cultural rebound" did not take place, but almost immediate cultural transplantation and adaptation did. Even these immigrant craftspersons adapted, incorporating American methods and designs, layering them on their traditional products and creating hybrids neither purely American nor European.

The half-timbered house, which had been popular in Germany since the sixteenth century, provides a good example of these phenomena. Half-timber, or *Fachwerk*, construction consists of a heavy frame of timbers with the spaces between the timbers filled with bricks or some other durable material. Initially, immigrant dwellings had been crude log buildings, or, as with the Lippe-Detmolders in Sheboygan County, even crude straw huts. But with the advent of better economic times and the reduction of the stress placed upon newcomers trying to secure basic shelter and food, settlers could build the more elaborate, time-consuming *Fachwerk* structures, which usually required the help of experts outside the family circle. An example of the two stages of immigrant housing appears on the Lueterbach farm east of Germantown in Washington County, where the original log cabin stands near a newer half-timber dwelling. But the half-timber buildings made in Wisconsin usually varied in some details from those at home, testifying to the modification and adaptation prompted by American materials, fashions, and local conditions.

In the rural Wisconsin countryside, Germans tended to build in the style of the urban or village half-timber house *(Deutsches Dorfhaus)* instead of the more complicated and more difficult to build rural farm dwelling *(Deutsches Bauernhaus)*. None of the hundreds of *Fachwerk* buildings surveyed in Wisconsin appears to have been built in the pure rural Germanic style. Two houses that exemplify how selective their builders were when returning to the older methods (or adapting them to American conditions and changing tastes) are the Schulz house, built in Dodge County in 1856, and the Koepsell house, built in Washington County about 1858. (In the 1970s, both houses were relocated to Old World Wisconsin, the outdoor ethnic museum operated by the State Historical Society of Wisconsin near Eagle in Waukesha County.)

The introduction of balloon-frame construction influenced all immigrant groups, the Germans included, for these buildings could be put up rapidly by relatively unskilled people. Balloon-frame barns gained quick popularity as well because they could be enlarged without excessive effort. At the same time, the spatial arrangement of farm buildings changed. The hollow square pattern, or *Vierkanthof,* common in German states, gave way to a single large barn with multiple functions. "Nowhere was the search for a more efficient organization of space more noticeable than in the new type of barn that became popular in the United States," notes one architectural historian, referring to the period following the 1860s.

Almost nowhere could Germans recreate Old Country models exactly, nor did a purely Germanic style of architecture catch on in the United States. (Actually, few Germans desired that it should.) An example of unsuccessful adaptation is seen in the efforts of a German rural community in Marathon County to establish a European-styled agricultural community, with a centralized location (a *dorf*) requiring farmers to travel between it and their fields. The experiment failed, as did others of its kind, because American space, land-division patterns, distance, and lack of transportation made them impractical.

But in at least two Wisconsin areas, adaptations of the centralized village pattern—the "*dorf* culture" found in heavily Catholic Bavaria—do exist. They are found in the so-called Holy Land of Calumet, Fond du Lac, and Sheboygan Counties between Lake Michigan and Lake Winnebago, and in northwestern Dane County—all solidly German Catholic farming districts. In each instance, devout Catholic settlers from appropriate German states appeared in the 1840s and 1850s. They established churches on rises of land and then set up farms around them, with the farm buildings clustered as near the church as possible. Blacksmith shops, taverns, and stores grew in arrays around the church. A family's fields were not scattered, as in Germany, and the distances traveled to them were not as inconvenient. The adaptations were successful, and their remnants are visible today in hamlets such as Roxbury and Martinsville in Dane County and Marytown and Johnsburg in Fond du Lac County.

An architectural Germanic imprint also found its way into several Wisconsin cities, especially Milwaukee and Madison. St. John's Cathedral in Milwaukee was designed by German-born Victor Schulte in the German *Zopfstil* style—a Baroque variant—while Frederick Velguth designed the Lutheran landmark church, Trinity Evangelical, in a gothic style. Henry Koch from Hanover developed a national reputation for his churches and courthouses and especially Milwaukee's city hall. The Germanic Pabst mansion in Milwaukee was the work of American-born George Bowman Ferry and his partner, Alfred C. Clas, a member of a Freethinking family from Sauk City. In Madison, German-born August Kutzbock designed the second state capitol building, the city hall, and the largest mansion in town, now Mansion Hill Inn, employing the German variant of the Romanesque revival style called *Rundbogenstil*. These Germanic influences on some of the state's most important buildings left a permanent impression on Wisconsin's appearance. But so did the work of German masons and builders of vernacular buildings.

Less tangible aspects of German cultural identity in Wisconsin include such matters as religious affiliation, family and marriage patterns, and foods. Churches were, and remain, a basic social institution, exerting a unifying effect, and religion was probably the most powerful social and spiritual force influencing the German immigrant. Family life was inextricably linked to religion, as one observer of German communities stated in 1888: "Many . . . live as they did in the old country. They conform to the general laws but keep up their church and family life as they would in Germany." Immigrants to Wisconsin from northern Germany were mainly Lutherans; from southern Germany, Catholics. Both groups had above-average rates of church attendance, and religious differences among Germans—sometimes bitter and protracted—tended to overshadow other ethnic and cultural differences within the Germanic community. Marriages between German Catholics and Lutherans were uncommon and usually resulted in at least one family's ostracizing a child and grandchildren. (The marriage partner who chose to convert to a spouse's religion was said to have "changed": "He changed for her.") Devout German Lutherans would even utter sighs of regret when a child married outside the family's synod into a different German Lutheran synod. Over time, of course, these betrayals of German birthright came to matter less and less within the Germanic community. Marriage statistics reflect a progressive change. In 1850, fewer than 10 percent of Germans married outside their ethnic group; by 1860, about 10 percent; 1870, about 20 percent; 1880, about 30 percent; and by 1920, almost 70 percent. But by 1920, the immigrant generations had shrunk in size, and it was hard to determine the marriage patterns of third-, fourth-, and fifth-generation German Americans.

While Germans may have distinguished among themselves as Catholics and Lutherans, Bavarians and Pomeranians, and so forth, the non-German Wisconsinite tended to lump all Germans into one category or to group them by religious affiliation. Regional and intradenominational distinctions meant nothing to most non-Germans.

Mutual insensitivity about cultural matters between Germans and non-Germans often led to disputes, some of them violent. The most regretted, and the most emblematic, may have been the lynching in 1855 of George DeBar, a Yankee who had physical and mental disabilities and who was watched over informally by a local businessman in West Bend, where the tragedy unfolded. DeBar worked occasionally for a German farmer, John Muehr, and Muehr owed him some wages. A misunderstanding arose and DeBar became enraged, knifing Muehr and his wife and killing their hired boy, Paul Winderling. The National Guard was called in to protect DeBar from the hundreds of Germans who came to the courthouse to witness his indictment. But the militiamen, too, were German, and they melted away from DeBar as he exited the courthouse. The mob seized him, beat him, dragged him through the town, and hanged him. The Germans clearly mistrusted the American system that it feared would free the Yankee murderer of a German immigrant. The Americans denounced the local Germans (who were in the majority by then) as "hideous monsters." And Germans and some Yankees inferred that the mob was composed of Roman Catholics of German background. The episode reveals the prejudices that simmered between and among ethnic groups and religious bodies all around Wisconsin in the nineteenth century.

Religious and political differences within the German community were the most pronounced and the most public differences, as demonstrated by the Bennett Law election and the DeBar lynching. But within the Germanic community itself there existed more subtle, less visible distinctions, as with regional foods and dialects. Their importance and persistence among Germans depended largely upon local circumstances. Where lots of persons from the same area concentrated in a Wisconsin neighborhood, they might persist for a long time. Where there were fewer Germans from disparate backgrounds, blending of Germans—pan-Germanism—began very soon. Over time, pan-Germanism has developed among almost all persons of German-speaking background in Wisconsin, whether they be Germans, Austrians, or German-speaking Bohemians and Hungarians. The blending incorporated various German and American institutions alike, creating a unique result that is neither German nor American. By the end of the twentieth century, the popular image of Wisconsin Germans, even among persons of German descent themselves, consisted of a man in lederhosen (originally Bavarian), a woman in dirndls (with no attention paid to regional variations in design), both eating bratwurst (a sausage that most modern European Germans consider a German-American invention), and drinking lager beer (originally a regional beer in northern Germany, later popularized and transformed in America). Germans from Germany find the image strictly American, not German.

Foodways are probably the first topic that comes up when Wisconsinites discuss ethnicity. What immigrants ate when they first arrived, however, cannot be determined with any certainty. Obviously in the early pioneer times, Germans, like all settlers, ate at a subsistence level. Gardens produced enough to go around, but luxuries such as meat were scarce. Rye, or "German corn," was a popular standby, although it was soon to be replaced by wheat, with which Germans began baking their bread. John Meidenbauer, writing to a relative in Germany, said: "Here in America we eat nothing but white bread . . . (always wheat bread, seldom rye, and even that is very white)." Another German, J. O. Kroehnke of New Holstein (who was elected justice of the peace in 1849), recorded in 1848 that he intended to plant rye in his fields "because the old dear black bread still tastes best, and in spite of the fact that we eat wheat bread, I prefer the rye bread." In New Holstein and elsewhere, and depending on district customs brought from Germany, bread was baked in outdoor ovens. Each family owned one, or if they did not, they carried the dough to a neighbor who did. Other Germans baked bread in indoor masonry bake ovens and in stove ovens, as iron stoves became commonly available in the mid-nineteenth century.

Cabbage was a fixture on many German tables, together with apples, cherries, potatoes, beets, and other fare from the kitchen garden. Wisconsin waterways abounding in fish and waterfowl, and woodlands thick with deer, bear, small game, and wild pigeons ensured a degree of variety at the family table. But a heavy, monotonous diet was the rule for most settlers, and sometimes there simply was not enough food to go around. In 1851 a German family recorded that for breakfast they had only "rye coffee, a piece of dry bread, and pumpkin syrup. Pumpkins were boiled, the mass strained, and the juice boiled down [for syrup]. It was not very appetizing! For Dinner [meaning the noon meal] we had bean soup or potato soup; for supper only rye coffee and bread spread with lard."

When life became more secure, Germans could revive the foods they liked best. Among the favorite dishes (again, depending on the specific Old County regional diets) were *Suelze,* or blood sausage, and *Gruetz Wurst,* a sausage made from buckwheat groats ground up with pork and pork blood. Another delicacy was *Schwarzauer,* a kind of stew made of goose and duck wings, livers, gizzards, and hearts cooked with apples, plums, blood, and dumplings. *Spickgans,* yet another favorite, consisted of the breast and shanks of goose immersed in brine for nine days and then smoked.

Bit by bit dietary customs faded, of course, and what had been everyday fare became special dishes for holidays, or forgotten altogether because of the American aversion (adopted by later generations of immigrants) for foods made of animals' internal organs. Recipes and knacks of preparation and butchering sometimes were lost in specific families and communities because they had been lodged in the memories of the immigrants who did not successfully pass them down to later generations. Still, food customs continue to survive, enshrined in locally published cookbooks and the occasional kitchen. When the State Historical Society invited Wisconsinites in 1974 to submit their old recipes, 900 responded, the largest number of them of German background, reflecting the predominance of Germanic persons in the state's population. Their submissions mirrored the wide range of cuisine within Germany. Foods (and the names for them) familiar in Schleswig-Holstein and in New Holstein in Wisconsin were unknown in equally German parts of Wisconsin where the original settlers had come from the southern or northeastern parts of Germany.

WHi(X3)6044

WHi(X3)36475

Robert Schilling (1843–1922), a German-born labor leader and reformer who played a key role in the Wisconsin Knights of Labor and the eight-hour-day movement.

Mathilde Franziska Anneke (1817–1884) fled her native Prussia after the revolutions of 1848 and began a fruitful career as a reformer, writer, and educator in Wisconsin.

WHi(X3)22821

Freethinkers *(Freie Gemeinde)* Congregation, Sauk City, 1902.

WHi(X3)12014

Downtown Milwaukee, c. 1900. At the turn of the century, the *Germania* declared itself the nation's largest German-language weekly newspaper.

WHi(X3)47997

WHi(X3)48914

Victor L. Berger (1860–1929), a native of Austria-Hungary, was a celebrated editor, reformer, and politician. In 1910 he became the first Socialist ever elected to Congress. This poster is from his senatorial campaign, 1918.

Meta (Schlicting) Berger (1873–1944) was not only her husband Victor's partner in Socialist politics but also a reformer in her own right. In 1909 she became the first woman elected to the Milwaukee school board.

Photo courtesy of Milwaukee County Historical Society

The staff of Victor L. Berger's Social-Democratic Publishing Company, Milwaukee, c. 1912.

VMA/SHSW

VMA/SHSD

Joseph Schlitz (1831–1875) of Mainz, Germany, took over the August Krug Brewery in 1856 and in 1874 began producing "the beer that made Milwaukee famous."

Valentin Blatz (1826–1894) was born in Bavaria and entered the brewing business in Milwaukee in 1848, the year of Wisconsin statehood.

VMA/SHSW

Phillip Best (1814–1869), also German-born, established the Empire Brewery in 1844 and eventually transferred leadership to his sons-in-law, Frederick Pabst and Emil Schandein.

WHi(X3)2231

WHi(X3)48032

Carl Schurz (1829–1906), an authentic "Forty-Eighter" who distinguished himself as a reformer, newspaperman, Civil War general, and cabinet officer.

Margarethe (Meyer) Schurz (1833–1876) was married to Carl Schurz in 1852 and in 1856 opened a Froebelite kindergarten—often described as the first such school in America.

WHi(X3)31375

Margarethe Schurz's kindergarten, the Lincoln School, in Watertown, Dodge County.

VMA/SHSW

Phillip H. Best's South Side Brewery (formerly Melm's Brewery), c. 1870. Like many other of Milwaukee's commercial and public buildings, Best's had a decidedly Teutonic cast.

VMA/SHSW

This grand Victorian residence with its neatly landscaped grounds was home to Frederick Pabst (1836–1904), successor to Phillip Best and one of Milwaukee's most famous brewers.

WHi(X3)21349

During World War I, patriotic fervor quickly turned into anti-German hysteria, marking an abrupt end to Wisconsin's pride in its "Germanness." This Liberty Loan parade was in Waupun, Dodge County, in 1918.

Milwaukee Journal photo/VMA

Today, vestiges of German-American culture survive in folk festivals, where food, music, and ethnic costume are the principal attractions. This *Pommern Tag* (Pomeranian Day) "heritage extravaganza" of 1985 is in Mequon, Ozaukee County.

JUST HOW GERMAN IS WISCONSIN?

The only way to begin to consider the question "How German is Wisconsin?" is to look at the U.S. decennial census returns beginning with 1850. In that decade, for the first time since 1790, the federal government asked people where they had been born. Already 38,064 residents (out of 305,391) in the two-year-old state of Wisconsin said they had been born in Germany. And that is where the problems begin, on two fronts: What is a German, and what about the American-born children of German speakers? The complications are seemingly endless. Germany did not exist as a unified nation until after 1870; census takers overlooked some persons; German-speaking children and grandchildren of the immigrant generation may sometimes appear only as Americans, when they are very much part of the Germanic community; each census asked questions about ethnicity and birthplace in somewhat different ways. These problems and inconsistencies mean that the accompanying tables and maps are at best a compromise. Nevertheless, the figures are the best that can be determined. In the future, perhaps, computer technology will foster improvements.

It is easy to see from the census figures that in 1990 Wisconsin was the most Germanic state in the Union. Some 2.6 million residents of 4.9 million in the state said that their ancestry was either primarily or secondarily German, for a percentage of 53.8—the highest of any state. And the states to the west were nearly as Germanic: Iowa, Minnesota, the Dakotas, and Nebraska are all just over or under 50 percent. As in Wisconsin, many communities in these states celebrate their Germanness, and their Germanic citizens have imposed certain distinguishing characteristics on them. For sheer numbers of Germans, the largest states of the union naturally have the most. But the pocket of German population strength in the Midwest bears an obvious relationship to the relatively large numbers and percentages of Germans found in the northern tiers of states: Illinois, Indiana, Michigan, Ohio, Pennsylvania, and New York, then skipping across the pocket to Montana, Colorado, Washington, and Oregon. The westward flow of both immigrant and migrant Germans began in the early 1800s in the port cities of the East and moved across the northern United States until it reached the Pacific. The area of most intense concentration occurred in the Midwest and centered in Wisconsin. This is logical for several reasons: transportation—since Wisconsin lies between Lake Michigan and the Mississippi River and has good railroad connections; good agricultural lands; forest resources; and an accident of timing—Wisconsin was just opening up at the same time Germany was giving up hundreds of thousands of persons largely for economic reasons. Wisconsin was therefore an easy choice for the German immigrant.

Besides geographical distribution of Germans, the census figures also demonstrate the inevitable dwindling of the immigrant generation. The numbers of German-born persons in Wisconsin peaked in 1890 at 259,819; the numbers of their children peaked in 1920 at 794,943. However, when it came to grandchildren and subsequent generations, not until the census of 1980 were American-born persons asked about their ancestry in general. And when they were asked, the results of natural increase among Wisconsin's Germans became obvious: The German proportion had grown remarkably, exceeding all others.

These figures may be somewhat misleading, because many Germanic persons in Wisconsin do not know where their ancestors came from. They know only that their ancestors spoke German (an unpopular language in Wisconsin because of the two world wars), so they leaped to a conclusion when they filled out the census questionnaires: We're German. In fact, German speakers in Wisconsin came from many places besides Germany: Austria, Switzerland, Luxembourg, Russia, Czechoslovakia, and Hungary. So the German figures have probably been inflated by ignorance—as they would have been inflated in other states as well.

Had natural increase occurred equally among all ethnic groups, it seems likely that the Germans would have continued in second place behind descendants of people who came from the British Isles (English, Irish, Scottish, Welsh). They predominated in the state's early years, and the Irish especially continued to immigrate. The cliché has it that both German Catholics and German Lutherans preferred large families—families larger than those of the original settlers who were mostly of English descent. If the cliché is true, it may be that Germans' reproductive rates surpassed most other ethnic groups' rates over several generations. But that is merely a hunch.

Another factor to be considered is intermarriage and multiple ethnic ancestries. (Most Americans have multiple ethnic ancestries.) How does an individual decide or choose first and second ancestries, as asked by the census in 1990? When three or four ethnic groups are almost equally represented in an individual's background, how does one pick? Some Wisconsinites with multiple ancestries, none of them dominant, may have chosen German because being in the German majority is now a comfortable choice in Wisconsin, more so than in any other state.

But while that may have been the case in 1990, it was certainly not the case for Wisconsin Germans between the onset of World War I in 1914 and the end of World War II in 1945. Those wars with Germany permanently changed Wisconsin's German community and hastened the Americanization process of many German Americans both in Wisconsin and elsewhere. Anti-German sentiment in the state, and nationally, put heavy pressures on Wisconsin Germans to assimilate more quickly and to rid themselves of the Germanisms that only a few years before had been marks of pride. No longer could Milwaukee bask in the glow of the phrase, "the German Athens." Overnight the compliment became an insult. In some parts of Wisconsin during World War I, people of German descent were physically attacked or publicly ridiculed; a New York newspaper published a map of Wisconsin with areas of suspected German sedition circled.

Even though Wisconsin's Germans constituted a near-majority population in Wisconsin, political, religious, and social differences within the community made it impossible for Germans to consolidate and react as a unified body. Such circumstances prompted Germans to put their public visibility on hold and to keep their internal disagreements increasingly to themselves. The lessons learned during World War I (1914–1918) were fresh in the mind of the Wisconsin Germanic community when World War II (1939–1945) erupted in Europe. In each war the immigrant community acquitted itself proudly, contributing sons and daughters to the armed services and donating liberally to Liberty Loan drives in the first war and war bond drives in the second. A desire to retain status required that Germans become more American, more law-abiding, more exemplary than any other group. And they needed to do so without drawing attention to themselves. Thus, overt Germanism in Wisconsin appears to have gone largely underground during and between the wars. This was not easy on the many Wisconsin Germans who had relatives in both the German and U.S. armies. Families were rent asunder; brothers fought brothers; cousins fought cousins.

Almost perversely, the steady loss to death of first-generation immigrants during this same period actually made Americanization slightly easier, since second-generation Germans usually had no trouble with English, even though they may have been raised in German-speaking households.

Occasionally names were changed, Schlesingerville becoming Slinger and Madison's German American Bank becoming the American Exchange Bank. It was better not to advertise German roots.

The transformation between the relative discomfort of being a German American in Wisconsin in 1945 and the comfort of being one in 1990 is a subject no scholar has yet explored. The postwar Marshall Plan, which provided American dollars to rebuild Germany, perhaps assisted in rehabilitating the overall reputation of Germany and German Americans. Indeed, Wisconsin's first-generation German American community grew after the war; many new German immigrants arrived in the state, but not in the astonishing numbers experienced a century before. These new immigrants gravitated to the existing, though often vestigial, German American organizations in the state and gave them new life. Immigrants soon dominated as officeholders and lent themselves to the ethnic festivals that cropped up everywhere in Wisconsin after World War II.

Slowly, pan-Germanism had become the rule in the Wisconsin, not only among Germans, but within the state as a whole. The German "tavern culture" and its definitions of popular entertainment gradually came to define Wisconsin itself, with the happy complicity of the northern and western Europeans who made up the rest of Wisconsin's population. Irish, English, Poles, Italians, Czechs, and, to a lesser extent, Norwegians, all brought with them a tradition of gathering at central places for drink, food, games, and socializing. The preponderance of Germans in Wisconsin somehow led to Wisconsin's identifying this culture as "Germanic," though it was merely European. Beer, schnapps, and brandy were the drinks of preference in the state; and non-Germans and Germans alike learned to play card games like sheepshead and skat and euchre. Nearly universal acceptance of these European characteristics seeped into the Wisconsin consciousness as German and came to define Wisconsin's reputation both within and outside the state.

All this occurred at a time when the state's Germanic community had begun to accept itself as a more or less unified entity. Political and religious differences meant less; use of the German language (especially dialects) became rare. You could not pick a German out of a crowd because of dress or speech, and everyone accepted the attributes of Germanic popular culture in Wisconsin as the normative culture. The passage of time helped make being German respectable again. It helped redeem the community internally and externally, as the horrors of the wars began to be forgotten and the older generations dwindled. By the 1990s it had once again become a good thing to be a German in Wisconsin.

That comfort zone, and the majority population figures, indicate how many changes Germans in Wisconsin have undergone since they first began arriving in the 1830s and 1840s. Then, differences in dialect, religion, customs, and philosophies meant everything. Some differences can still be detected here and there in food preferences, special dishes, public festivals, religious observations, turns of phrase, German slang, games, individual household habits, architecture, some place names, and stereotypical behaviors like the stubbornness attributed to almost all persons of European background. These survivals have been the subject of museum exhibits, restorations, and scholarly monographs. They are something to show off, although they bear almost no relationship to everyday life of the average Wisconsinite of German descent.

Of course, variations continue to exist within and among Wisconsin German communities. Homogeneity applies only in the broadest sense, and adaptation took many forms as Germans felt their way toward becoming Americans. The modern visitor from Germany usually does not see much that resembles the Old Country in what Wisconsinites call German. They visit Wisconsin to see what German Americans have made of the place; but they soon identify Wisconsin as American, not German. The visitor readily accepts the fact that, for the most part, persons in Wisconsin of German descent have become homogenized pan-Germans. Descendants of immigrants, now commonly counting back seven or eight generations, have created a new kind of German: the American German. German visitors are even more keenly aware than American Germans of the impact two world wars had on how people feel about them. Without saying so, they probably understand how the wars homogenized the Wisconsin German community and perhaps hastened Americanization. Other ethnic groups in Wisconsin—notably the Swiss and Norwegians—have made more of an industry of their ethnicity than the majority Germans.

Because of the wars, and despite their numbers and their consequent opportunities to have retained a distinctive ethnicity, Germans have succeeded more at assimilation and Americanization than have most other nineteenth-century, non-English-speaking ethnic groups in Wisconsin. Their initial story after their first arrival may have been one of transplanting Germany to Wisconsin. Now their story has become one of adaptation and transformation. The first-generation survivals are a pleasant, poignant reminder of where Wisconsin's Germans in Wisconsin came from and how far they have come since. By the early twenty-first century, the state's Germanic majority population is far more American than German.

Nonetheless, hosts of Germanic names testify to the importance of Germans in the state, to their ceaseless toil to create farms and businesses, to their continuing influence on all aspects of Wisconsin life—not as immigrants, but as full-fledged, fully integrated citizens. The German stamp on Wisconsin endures in the state's commitment to efficient agriculture, hard work, education, culture, and to good citizenship and political freedom—all of which were an integral part of the German immigrant's baggage.

THE LONG JOURNEY
OF THE DIEDERICHS FAMILY,
1847–1848

What follows is the latter part of a long document—part letter, part journal—describing the journey of the family of Johann Friederich Diederichs from Elberfeld, Germany, the ensuing ocean voyage from Bremerhaven to New York, and from there to Milwaukee and Manitowoc, during the year in which Wisconsin attained statehood. Originally translated by Emil Baensch, the entire document was published in the Wisconsin Magazine of History *in 1924 (vol. 7: 218–237, 350–368). It is a both vivid and touching document, a mixture of piety, wonder, and practical advice for others. Although little is known about the subsequent history of this particular family, it seems safe to say that Diederichs's account of immigration and settlement mirrors the experience of thousands of other new-comers from the German states and elsewhere in Europe.*

THE OVERSEAS JOURNEY

Milwaukee

Jan. 3, 1848

. . . On the 19th of August we left our dear [friend] Bicker [in Bremerhaven] and toward evening went on board, since it was to be expected that we would get under sail early in the morning. And so it turned out. Friday, the 20th, at 4 o'clock in the morning, we started, and with us 8 or 10 other ships, all under full sail, so that our dear German fatherland will soon vanish from our sight, but never from our hearts. . . . [Monday the 23d] Sea-sickness is in full swing, and it is amusing to see how big, strong men writhe and choke and roar, in order to pay their tribute, while children and women escape much easier. . . . [Wednesday the 24th] This morning there were earnest remonstrances to the captain on account of the extremely bad meals, which are sometimes burnt, then too salty, and again unclean. . . . [Thursday the 25th] Today the first lice on the ship were discovered, which has filled us with anxiety and fear. . . . Only a few days at sea and how bored we are with life on a ship! Could we but once more drink water to the full in Louise street, how grateful we would be; how glad we would be to see some fish etc. for a change! . . . [Tuesday the 31st] Stormy. Of course, the sailors laugh at our idea of a storm, but it fully satisfies me and I would gladly refrain from any closer acquaintance. The bow of the ship dives deep into an abyss and the waves meet high above our heads; in addition, it rains and freezes and no one is able to stand without holding on to something. O, if it would only come to pass, as the captain stated today, that we will arrive in New York before the end of September. . . . [Friday, September 3d] Today it's 14 days that we are on the sea—if we had only reached our goal! In Bremen we had bought some apples and today we exchanged some of them for eggs; a Swiss lady gave us some flour, we added two ship-biscuits, and then six pancakes were baked, which furnished us a royal meal. . . . [Sunday the 5th] This is the day of the Lord. We have no lack of sermons on the ship,—two daily. . . . Sundays we have rice and smoked meat, but this is generally so salty that one cannot eat it. Bacon is still the best meat. On the whole the meals are miserably poor; I would not complain if they were only eatable, but under existing circumstances—well, it will all pass over and we will endure patiently. . . . [Friday the 17th] Clear, pleasant day. Wind like yesterday [north-northwest, "not exactly favorable"]. How dissatisfied I am and how often I ask, why does the Lord not give us good winds? Does he not know that I am on the ship? Does he not know that my means are meager and that I must necessarily have my hut ready before winter? . . . [Sunday the 26th] Today it is five weeks that we have been at sea and with the little wind we have a good opportunity to meditate on the journey passed. . . . About five o'clock the wind changed, and that favorably. O, would but the Lord keep this up for 10 to 14 days! [Friday, October 1st] Although today, with rainy weather, the wind is favorable, yet we have postponed our hopes of arrival to the 4th or 5th instant. Perhaps the anniversary day of my birth will also be the day of our arrival. . . . [Tuesday the 12th] The wind is stronger, we are moving rapidly forward, and expect the pilot on board today. Everybody is on the lookout. Noon: The wind is growing stronger, almost stormy, and since no pilot has yet appeared, the captain intends to haul in the sails so that during the night we may remain far enough from land and have no mishap to fear. 4 o'clock P.M.: On the far distant horizon a small sail appears and every one is anxious to know whether it is the pilot boat. I am too fearful to believe it. Yes! It is! Through his spyglass the captain recognizes it by its shape; it is the pilot boat! . . . Ever wilder the ship courses through the high waves—but the pilot stands fast at his post and calmly and firmly faces the storm. Brothers, I then acquired admiration for the American pilot! At 9 o'clock, it was said, we would see the lighthouses, and so it turned out. I was on deck most of the time; everything was new to me, and the time seemed long until I could see my new fatherland. The anchors were cast and we lay at the mouth of the Hudson. . . . [Wednesday the 13th] At daybreak we were all on deck to see the land and gradually, on both sides, it appeared through the dawn. What a sight! There it lies, the land in which I and mine shall hereafter live, where my remains will rest. . . . All, all, all, is with Thee, Thou true God!—Soon the anchors are lifted and toward 10 o'clock in the morning we at last enter the harbor, where soon a crowd of German leeches come on board, one knowing of a good tavern, another of good work, a third this, a fourth that. However, it seems to me that the Germans have in time become too wise to be fooled by them. After our arrival we went on land as soon as possible, since our baggage was not to be delivered until the following day. . . .

THE WAY WEST

. . . At Buffalo we looked for a steamboat to Milwaukee, and again I arranged for the 4½ persons, at 4 dollars, furnishing our own meals, which, however, are not very expensive, for as a rule they consist of bread, cheese, and water from Lake Michigan. On this trip, which is usually made in 5 or 6 days, we spent 11 days, and I must designate this as the hardest and most dangerous part of our journey from Europe, on the one hand because we felt ourselves wholly in the hands of the careless American, and on the other hand because Lake Michigan is in constant unrest and agitation. Several weeks ago a steamboat [the *Phoenix*] was destroyed by fire near Sheboygan, due to the carelessness of a machinist who had become drunk at Manitowoc, and 250 poor immigrants were sacrificed and only 44 were saved. One can imagine the sad plight of these people, suffering this horrible death within sight of Sheboygan, where most of them intended to land and expected to find the end of their hard and troublesome journey. In Washington [Port Washington] I met a young man whose father, mother, 2 brothers, 2 sisters, and 2 sisters-in-law had lost their lives in the fire, and only he and his wife and child were saved, with nothing but the clothes on their bodies.

The hand of our faithful God brought us safely into Milwaukee at 2 o'clock in the morning, and after we had come into possession of all our baggage, which was not until noon, we bade a sad farewell to our dear John (the Christian sailor who came with us from Bremen), to Wink, who has decided to go to Chicago, and to Brauer, who intends to go to St. Louis by way of

Chicago. We had made the great journey together, had come to know one another well, had shared joy and sorrow, and hence the separation was painful, my wife being unable to restrain her tears. I consoled her as well as I could, told her we would soon meet new friends, would find Kohl and Flertzheim, and promised to look them up as soon as we had had our meal. I did this, and first found Flertzheim, whose joy upon my entering his room was overflowing, and whose wife, if I had not protested, would at once have gone for my family, although she had not yet inquired where we were quartered. She wanted us all to drink coffee with them, and when I told her that since we left Bremen my wife had drunk none and could not drink the American coffee, she promised to make a genuine German, Elberfelder coffee which we would surely like. I now brought my family, and my wife feasted royally. Since the American only half roasts the coffee, it takes considerable time to get used to it. After the coffee we went together to see Kohl, and arrived just as his wife was telling a neighbor that Schrey and Diederichs might be expected any moment. How great was the pleasure of our meeting again I need not tell you, and during our entire stay in Milwaukee the two families vied with each other to show us their love and friendship. Both of them are prospering, and neither has any desire to return to Europe again.

Since I wanted to go out from here looking for land, I rented a room the next day for one month at 3 dollars (a cheaper one, where we could store our boxes, was not to be had); and since we live with a German butcher my wife can get all the fat she needs and even more, to store up for future use. Usually we have Panas with our coffee in the morning, vegetables at noon, and coffee in the evening. Occasionally we alternate at noon with meat, which is very cheap here. Beef is 3 or 4 cents per pound, pork 4 to 5 cents (a cent equals 5 Pfennige), a barrel of wheat flour, first quality, 196 pounds, 3¾ dollars, or 1½ cents per pound (7½ Pfennige), and potatoes, which, by the way, are sometimes very poor, 3 shilling or 5 silver Groschen per bushel (about 3¾ Scheffel). I bought a stove for 15½ dollars and must admit that one can't imagine anything more practical; there are 4 openings in it besides a bake-oven, wherein we bake our fine bread, and in addition we received, included in the above price, 2 iron pots, 3 iron pans, 2 tin pans for baking bread, 1 tin kettle holding 4 pails of water, 1 tin teakettle, 1 tin skimmer, and 1 dipper.

Thus far had we come with God's help, and our first anxiety was to obtain some land. In order that the poor also may find it possible to own land, the government allows every American citizen to claim 160 acres—that is, the government grants him a year's time to pay for it. One receives a certificate from the General Land Office stating that he has claimed 160 acres according to law. Then he must live on the land, build a house, clear and sow, and a year later, on the day and hour, pay for it. But if this is not done the land is forfeited with all improvements made thereon. Then, too, any one who knows that the land has been claimed, and not bought, may go to the Land Office and cover the land; that is, he deposits 100 or 200 dollars for 80 or 160 acres, with a declaration that he desires the land if the claimant does not pay on the day and the hour; in that case the latter does not receive one cent for his labor, improvements, or expenses. Congress land—that is, such as may be bought from the government for $1\frac{1}{4}$ dollars per acre—was not to be had within 40 to 60 miles of Milwaukee, and what there was of it, in second and third hands, costs at least from ten to twenty dollars per acre. From this can be seen how one can speculate in lands, especially when they lie near large cities and when wealthy immigrants are arriving daily who buy these lands at any price named.

SETTLING IN THE NEW LAND

. . . After searching for several days we finally found some suitable land, 9 miles from Manitowoc, 7 miles from Rapids, and 20 to 22 miles from Sheboygan. It was decided to build a house on each 160 acres, the same to serve as a temporary residence, and later, when the land should be divided, to be used as a stable. For the time being we were quartered with our nearest neighbor, Hobecker, and started to work immediately—cut down trees for logs, carried them on our shoulders through the snow, which had fallen in the meantime, to the building site, and continued this work from Monday until Saturday, all week long.

If you, my dear ones, could have seen me—how I arose in the morning from my bed of cornstalks with a block of wood for a pillow, partook of half baked or half burnt, sour, dry bread and black coffee without sugar, for breakfast; at noon dry bread and black coffee again, with turnip soup, and the same in the evening—then, I am sure, you would have been nearer tears than laughter. But in these days of hard work, privations, and the overcoming of all disgust, I have found what strength and joyousness come from the knowledge that we are in the path of the Lord. . . . A Bushman having slaughtered a cow, we have for several days had meat twice daily. . . .

And now, my dear ones, I am a farmer, have eighty acres or 128 Prussian Morgens of land, and livestock consisting of a dog and a cat. A sturdy peasant—eh? The dog is indispensable on account of the cattle, the cat on account of the mice, which are numerous in the woods. I have fine, rolling land, sloping toward the morning sun, with trees slender and tall, such as oaks of three varieties, sugar or maple, beech, elm, ash, walnut trees, plum trees, etc. Indeed, if I could do as I wished, I should forthwith give you a present of 15,000 to 20,000 dollars; for Pflieps, who is a carpenter, tells me that if any one would pay me $30,000 for my lumber laid down in Elberfeld, he would have a splendid bargain. You may ask what we do with it. Into the fire with the soundest, finest trees, three or four feet in diameter! Into the fire with them if we do not happen to need them for fences or some other purpose. Through the middle of my property flows a little creek, about the size of the Lohrmuehler Creek near Neviges, giving me a layout for the finest pastures. In short, my land is so pretty and its location is so excellent that all my friends insist, and I myself admit, that the best portion fell to me, and although Pflieps offered me $25 if I would trade with him, I will not do so but will keep what the Lord has allotted to me.

When once I have my land secure, then I shall work my way through all right. But how the money goes you may learn from the following: Just now I need a barrel of flour and cannot buy one for less than $7; then I still need four hundred feet of boards, which I must buy, for I cannot afford to saw them myself, since I dare not lose an hour from clearing the land and preparing it for seeding. The more I have for planting and seeding the more shall I have at harvest. I must have potatoes to plant, wheat, oats, and corn to sow, and must have some to live on until harvest. Whatever, therefore, is not absolutely necessary, must be deferred and done without. Hence I dare not think of cows and oxen, necessary and profitable though they would be. But I am sure that if I clear and partly plant from six to eight of my eighty acres by summer, I could easily get from four to five hundred dollars from the same. Then I could pay for the land and have three or four hundred dollars left. But I am heartily tired of roving about and long for rest. If it is the Lord's will, I shall die here, and I hope that such will be His will.

Farms which are well situated and whereon enough has been cleared and planted to support a family are very rapidly rising in price, for during the summer immigrants who have money are arriving nearly every day, and would rather buy a farm than settle on Congress land in the midst of the woods. I venture to say that since there is no Congress land available in or near Milwaukee, the trend of immigration will be toward this place and Sheboygan. This is advantageous to us, for it increases the value of our land and makes it easier to sell our produce.

Follow me now, my dear ones, in my daily work, as it has thus far appeared, and let me lead you into our family life and present to you a picture of our activities and contentment.

Not counting small injuries to our hands, caused by the hard work and rigorous cold, we are all well and happy, for which we cannot sufficiently thank our dear Lord. We arise at daybreak in the morning, about six or half past six, read the Word of God together, and drink coffee, with milk—no, no! Milk? A farmer such as I am does not yet have that, but, as head of the family, I have sugar, which is very cheap here, and probably next year will cost us nothing, for then we can tap it ourselves. With the coffee we have very good bread. With butter perhaps? Where there is no milk there can be no butter, and we should have to be satisfied with dry bread if mother had not saved some bacon fat into which we can dip it.

Directly after breakfast we begin working, and since Kohl is still busy preparing doors and windows for the house, I, with Fred and Carl, each with ax on shoulder, go out to clear the land about the house; we chop the branches off the trees and shorten the trunks as much as possible so that they will not be too heavy to carry or roll to the wood-pile. That is no easy work, and the higher the pile of logs, brush, and chips is, the better it is and the merrier will it burn.

Towards noon we return to the house, and mother has white beans with bacon, or bean soup with bacon, or rice soup with bacon, or barley soup with bacon, or flour dumplings with bacon, which last combination usually constitutes our Sunday meal. Potatoes, vegetables, or beef are for the present not to be found with us, and just now mother reports that there is no more barley left; hence in the future we shall have one course less, and the good housewife will have that much less trouble deciding what to cook.

Then back to work again, accompanied by the good mother and Mrs. Kohl to aid us as well as they can, and after sundown we all repair to the house and treat ourselves again to black coffee, dry bread, and sometimes bacon. Then we read a chapter from the Bible and gather about the warm stove, chat about you and others, venture guesses that this one will follow us and the other also, and that this one will fit in here, and the other not. Often I am so exhausted from the hard day's work that I am too tired to smoke a pipe, for to begin such work at the age of 44 years, and not lose courage, is some undertaking! But I must acknowledge and praise the faithful assistance of my Fred and Carl, and I hope their obedience and diligence will yet bring us much joy. They, as well as their two sisters, have grown considerably. . . .

You will next ask: "Is it really good in America, and are you not sorry that you have gone there?" And I can give you the answer, from my full conviction and in accordance with the truth: "Yes, it really is good here, as well for people with money as for those that have none, if the latter are capable and industrious workmen or mechanics—among whom I include carpenters, especially joiners, shoemakers, blacksmiths, tailors, tinsmiths, etc." The mechanics receive at once, if they are shop foremen, twelve shillings, $1.50 per day, without board, as the owner of a shop in Milwaukee informed me—which, by the way, is said to be one of the worst places for mechanics in America. But every one must see to it that he is thoroughly competent in his line, otherwise it will go hard with him if he must work with Americans. If, however, one intends to become a farmer and has money to buy a farm, he will find here a pleasant life and an assured future awaiting him; daily the finest estates, with cattle and all things that belong thereto, are being sold at from eight hundred to four or five thousand dollars, according as the farm is large or small, much or little cleared, near or far from cities or landing places. As for one who has no money, he will do best first to hire out to a farmer. He can then easily lay by fifty dollars within half a year, and with that he can buy 40 acres of Congress, that is, unimproved, land. Of course he must thoroughly exert himself that his land be made arable and, if he begin in the spring, that it be fruitful the same year; but after he has passed this first year he need have no more anxiety as to subsistence, and ere three or four years have elapsed he will be able to take part of his harvest to any of the numerous markets and exchange it for money or victuals.

As far as hunting is concerned, let no one entertain any false notions, for while there is plenty of game, the newly arrived farmer has more important things to attend to than to spend his time hunting; for he must direct all his activities to clearing and building, and think of other matters only when he has attained a secure position. Self-dependence and endurance must not be wanting in immigrants, especially in those without means. Whoever is faint-hearted and cannot conform to any condition in life, had better not come. The word "distress" is unknown to the Americans. As far as I am concerned, I can, hand on heart, declare naught else but that I thank the Lord that I am here and regret that I did not come sooner; and when my memory turns to many among you and I reflect how, with your means, you could live here, I am sorry, humanly speaking, not to have you here. . . .

SPRING IN WISCONSIN

. . . We had a mild winter this year, and only a few days when the snow could withstand the sun; it rained but little and I do not believe that on the whole we had fourteen days when it was not possible to work. As a general rule all natural phenomena in America are on a grand scale. When it does storm, you hear a crashing in the forest as if there were cannon booming; trees are uprooted and fall with thunderous din upon others, taking their branches with them. During such a storm no one ventures into the woods. Altogether, there is a strangeness about the "Bush." Of paths there is no thought and it is therefore easy to get lost, and one is not able to find his way again unless he takes as his guide the sun by day and the moon by night, if they be visible. Therefore every one must consider it his duty, before retiring, to step outside and listen, to hear whether any one is calling; that this practice is of benefit was recently proved to us by August Poetz, who was coming from the Rapids, had been delayed and lost his way, and would have been forced to camp in the woods over night if his call had not reached me. We are the outermost settlers here, and how far to the south and west of us there are people living we do not know. A. Poetz and Grauman, of Iserlohn, are now here to build a log house on their forty-acre tract located about ten minutes from us; Poetz, however, with wife and children will remain in Milwaukee, intending to come here after the opening of navigation. The family has thus far not prospered, since work is scarce in Milwaukee this winter; I believe, however, it will be better next summer in Manitowoc or the Rapids, where there is much building.

As yet Wisconsin has very few churches and schools, for the state is just beginning to flourish; but Milwaukee, after eleven years' existence, already has 15,000 inhabitants, some twenty churches—seven of them Lutheran, and nearly all differing among themselves. It seems as though our state will in time become predominantly German, for my countrymen already constitute a majority of the population and in Milwaukee there is more German than English spoken. . . .

My dear wife has planted the garden; I have seeded a tract with corn and beans, and, God willing, shall plant potatoes and sow corn and oats this week—I am writing this on May 15th. With Fred and Carl I am now busy building a fence around the cleared land, which will be finished tomorrow and whose purpose is to keep swine and other animals off the land. My two boys afford me genuine joy, and I assure you that if I did not have them I should never get through, for it is in fact no trifling matter, and many a person, if he knew what it means to be a farmer, would consider it ten times before he left Europe. However, I do not for a moment regret that I am here, because I am convinced (humanly speaking) that my future will brighten, although my children will have the real benefit of it.

The first year is, of course, the hardest, when everything must be purchased; yet, as an example, I am now raising all our provisions and hope to have some for sale next year; every year more land will be cleared and consequently more harvested. To tell the truth, I must say that whoever has money and the inclination to be a farmer can do no better than to come here; and when I think of some of my friends who are daily putting their little money into risky speculations, I am moved to exclaim: "Oh, if you but knew that, with the smallest capital, you could gain a competence here that would assure the safest, simplest, and most quiet life!"

He who settles on wild land should have about $500; but for $2000 one can at any time buy the finest farms, with all livestock and with provisions for one year (for people and cattle), and I should like to know what more can be desired. Likewise in money matters—the lowest interest is twelve per cent, with the best security; also much money is to be earned in trade, and if I had the means I should import some ribbons, sewing implements, and buttons, and feel sure of great profits. Otherwise it is necessary to have for trade a knowledge of the English language and of the best sources of supply. Finally, I want to report that since yesterday our woods are full of pigeons, coming in great swarms, covering this entire region; they are very palatable and we could shoot them at our pleasure if we only had the time for it. There is a tradition current here that the region where the pigeons appear will that same year be fully occupied by human beings, which, if that should really occur here, would be great luck for us; for then, naturally, our property would rise greatly in value. And now, to the faithful God, before whom we shall all be united again, may you all be committed.

FOR FURTHER READING

Because of Germans' pervasive influence on Wisconsin's development, their story has been woven into the standard histories of Wisconsin as well as being the subject of separate monographs, many of them in German. The principal English-language sources include the six-volume *History of Wisconsin* series (1973–2000) published by the State Historical Society (see especially the bibliographies at the back of each volume); numerous articles in the *Wisconsin Magazine of History* (whose decennial indexes provide easy access); and the publications of the Milwaukee County Historical Society, notably the *Historical Messenger* and *Milwaukee History.* Of special interest in the *Wisconsin Magazine of History* are Joseph Schafer's five pioneering articles, "The Yankee and the Teuton in Wisconsin," appearing in volumes 6 and 7. Two other pioneering works are by Kate Everest Levi, "How Wisconsin Came by Its Large German Element," in volume 12 (pp. 299–334) of the *Wisconsin Historical Collections,* and "Geographical Origin of German Immigration to Wisconsin," in volume 14 of the same series (pp. 341–393). The Milwaukee County Historical Society arranged the translation and publication of an important group of immigrant letters: Louis Frederick Frank, *German-American Pioneers in Wisconsin and Michigan: The Frank-Kerler Letters, 1849–1865* (1971). Kathleen Neils Conzen has analyzed Milwaukee's German and Irish communities in *Immigrant Milwaukee, 1836–1860: Accommodation and Community in a Frontier City* (Cambridge, Massachusetts, 1976). A useful survey that includes Germans, *The Immigrant Experience in Wisconsin* (Boston, 1985), was written by La Vern J. Rippley, who also has written *The German-Americans* (Boston, 1976).

THE AUTHOR

Richard H. Zeitlin was born in New York City in 1945. He did his undergraduate work at Queens College and earned both a master's degree and a doctorate in history at the University of Wisconsin, the latter in 1973. He worked for Old World Wisconsin, the State Historical Society's outdoor ethnic museum, between 1973 and 1977. Zeitlin became director of the Wisconsin Veterans Museum in 1982, a position which he held until his death in 2008.

INDEX